"God is Love. We are made in the image and likeness of God. Our goal is to grow into a fully human person capable of love and being loved. A difficult and lofty task for anyone. Martin Rymarz has written a truthful and motivating account of his struggle to achieve this goal. I think all who read his account will find it inspiring and helpful."

Bishop Thomas Gumbleton—Humanitarian, Peace Activist and Retired Auxiliary Bishop Detroit, MI

"One man's fascinating journey from young adult to maturity. On the way he has found a deep relationship with God and those closest to him"

Sister Irene Nowell—Biblical Scholar and Benedictine Sister of Mt. Saint Scholastica Monastery in Atchison, Kansas Author of—Women in the Old Testament; Pleading, Cursing, Praising: Conversing with God through the Psalms; Wisdom: The Good Life: Wisdom Literature and the Rule of Benedict; Sing a New Song: The Psalms in the Sunday Lectionary

"Few people have experienced the rich and varied faith journey of Martin Rymarz. Enduring an impoverished childhood, the divorce of his parents, and his own troubled relationships; traveling the world for a corporate job and later roaming the country in an RV; then studying Islam, Buddhism, and Jainism before making his way back to the Catholicism of his birth, Rymarz has much to teach us about the universal journey into love. While his life experience is singular, we can't help but see the narrative of our own lives in this beautifully written and affecting memoir. An important book about faith as lived in the 21st century."

Judith Valente, author of—How To Live: What The Rule of St. Benedict Teaches Us About Happiness, Meaning and Community; Atchison Blue: A Search for Silence, A Spiritual Home and A Living Faith; and The Art of Pausing: Meditations for the Overworked and Overwhelmed

ISBN 978-1-64670-693-8 (Paperback)
ISBN 978-1-64670-694-5 (Digital)

Copyright © 2020 Martin Rymarz
All rights reserved
First Edition

All rights reserved. No part of this publication may be reproduced, distributed, or transmitted in any form or by any means, including photocopying, recording, or other electronic or mechanical methods without the prior written permission of the publisher. For permission requests, solicit the publisher via the address below.

Covenant Books, Inc.
11661 Hwy 707
Murrells Inlet, SC 29576
www.covenantbooks.com

JOURNEY *into* LOVE
One Man's Global Journey of Faith

MARTIN RYMARZ

To my wife and kids,
I love you with all my heart, and this is dedicated to
you. Thank you always for your love and support.

CONTENTS

Acknowledgment 11
Preface..13

Chapter 1: Class Struggle 15
    Integrating Cultures...15
    Primary Education...18
    Racial Harmony 20
    Altered States..22
    Midwestern Roots..24
Chapter 2: God Is Always Present 27
    Faith as a Youth 27
    Religious Influences...28
Chapter 3: Fatherhood 32
    Where Are You, Dad?..32
    Adrift into Manhood...34
    An Unknown Gift 35
Chapter 4: A Child of Divorce 39
    Not Fitting In..39
    Gender Roles..41
    Driving Mrs. Thrasher...44
    Living in the Eye of the Storm 45
    Work as an Escape...47
    First Experience With Racism.................................50
Chapter 5: Married Life 52
    Marrying Young..52
    Shacking Up...55
    Getting Hitched 57

Chapter 6: Children 60
    New Life 60
    A Son 63
    A Second Son 65
    Growing Up 66
Chapter 7: On the Move 69
    Relocating for Work 69
    Rajun Cajuns 72
    A Wondering Soul 74
    Go West, Young Man 78
    Have Suitcase, Will Travel 81
Chapter 8: The Fall from Grace 88
    Hiding from God's Light 88
    Looking in the Mirror 98
Chapter 9: The Journey Back 101
    A Real and Deepened Faith 101
    Scripture—The Word of God 105
    Sr. Mary—A Voice of Compassion 106
    Third Orders 111
    Diocesan Life 113
    Ministry—Hospice, Chaplaincy 116
Chapter 10: Mystical Experiences 127
    The Devil Is in the Details and My Hallway 127
    Healing Seminar—Gift of Prophecy 130
    Speaking in Tongues 132
    Ghosts in the Machine and My Dreams 133
    Silent Retreats at Manresa 138
    Experiences after Receiving Eucharist 141
Chapter 11: A More Mature Faith 145
    Spiritual Direction 145
    Seminary Experience 149
    Studies of Different Faiths 151
    Thomas Merton and Bede Griffith 158
    Silent Retreats 161
Chapter 12: Benedictine Spirituality and Balance 163
    Benedict and His Rule 163

    Oblate Life 167
    St. Benedict Monastery..168
    Mount St. Scholastica 169
Chapter 13: A Marriage of Equals 172
    A Final Chance at Love..172
    Christ as the Center of Our Marriage 178
    Twelve Steps to Happiness.......................................180
    Codependency Issues..183
Chapter 14: The Journey Continues 186
    Leaving the Corporate World 186
    Hitting the Road 198
    Going Back to Work...215
    Volunteering..222
    Death in Community..229
    Journeying into Love 230

ACKNOWLEDGMENT

I am grateful for all those along my journey who have lovingly taken time to teach, coach, cajole, and correct me on my path. For those that have provided mentorship, spiritual direction, and love, I am forever grateful. May this book capture some of the wisdom you have provided and reflect the love that you have shared with me.

PREFACE

It must have been ninety degrees outside; at least that's what it felt like when John-Martin and his brother Mark entered the Blind Pig on Saturday July 22, 1967. The Blind Pig was known to many as a cool place to beat the sweltering Detroit summer heat and to quench one's thirst with some cool liquid fire. Unbeknownst to John-Martin and Mark, two Vietnam veterans who were home between tours of duty, that night the Pig, an illegal after-hours club, was to be raided by the Detroit police department as they sought to close down these illegal establishments. At 3:30 a.m., as the temperature outside finally started to cool down, the racial temperature rose off the scale as a white police force both disbursed and arrested the largely black crowd inside the Pig. As tempers escalated and bottles were hurled at the white officers, the start of one of America's deadliest race riots had begun. After four days of rioting, over seven thousand arrests, and forty-three deaths, order was tenuously restored, and America had come to see the ugly stains of racism once again.

Into this political and racial climate in the burgeoning Rust Belt, an eldest son was born out of wedlock, seventy-five miles north of Detroit, to a Catholic mother just barely out of high school herself. Though the very first signs of oxidation had just begun to show on the area of the Midwest that would become to be known as the Rust Belt, the changing racial, social, and economic climate would form the basis of this young man's perspective from a young age. This young man, the author of the book you hold in your hands now, would be formed by his Catholic faith, racial movements of the times, and social status as the adopted son of a blue-collar auto worker.

Through the grace of God, the author has had numerous transfiguring and unforgettable life experiences that others may find interesting and beneficial. For those just starting to raise children and struggling with the issues of adulthood, marital fidelity, making faith something more than a gift passed down from another generation, the hope is that this book may provide insights to help steer around some of the avoidable mistakes that are possible along the way. The author's prayer is that the mistakes and the resulting lessons learned from them will be like so many stepping stones that may be placed along the path of your journey and that they may help you along the way.

This book may also help to illuminate how God forgives and offers grace, love, and happiness to the most repetitive sinners. A few glimpses of what this love looks and feels like to the author are shared. Finally, as we continue to live in a world that through technology grows smaller and more diverse, we find ourselves more disconnected from our fellow man. Shared insights into the common mystical experience that we all live, whether we are cognizant of it or not, may show that through love and respect, a oneness of unity and being is possible.

CHAPTER 1
Class Struggle

He defends the cause of the fatherless and the widow, and loves the foreigner residing among you, giving them food and clothing.
—Deuteronomy 10:18

Integrating Cultures

Being born out of wedlock and never knowing my real father was certainly not the plan my mother had for her firstborn child. As a waitress working to make some money to help her widowed mother on the farm, my mother was hard working from a young age. Perhaps this desire for something immediately better than the life she had was what motivated my mother to show interest in Jerry, my biological father. A good-looking man with a gift for conversation and a good sense of humor, he had promises of a better life that were a siren song for someone looking for just that. Whatever promises or dreams that were shared were quickly broken when Jerry found out there would be a third person entering the family portrait in July of 1966. Before I was born, Jerry had left town as quickly as he had entered and was literally never to be heard from again by either my mother or me. Being born to a single mother in the mid-1960s to a strongly Catholic family was not something that people just shrugged their shoulders at and moved on. There was tremendous guilt and pressure on my mother. Thus, from before the time I was born, my grandmother played a key role in my life.

Within the first year of my life, my mother had met another man, Leonard, who would look beyond the stigma of the single mom and would marry her and adopt me as his son. Leonard was also raised in a very strict Catholic family. His parents were first generation Polish immigrants and were, I'm sure, not pleased that their oldest son had chosen to marry a country girl who had already had a son.

Leonard was raised and educated through Catholic schools. His parents had dreams for him to become a dentist or some other professional career. Leonard's father, Stanley, was a salaried production line supervisor for General Motors. Living and working in the Flint area in the greater part of the twentieth century meant there was a very good chance you either worked for General Motors or for a supplier to General Motors. Like all fathers who dream of their children doing something better than the career they had, Leonard's early career direction of dentist or professional was a reflection of his parents' desires for their children to achieve the American dream, whatever that meant for first generation immigrants.

The cultural and social shock to my adopted grandparents must have been significant when they found out that their oldest son had chosen to drop out of dental school, marry a single mother, and then, most troubling of all, work for General Motors as an hourly assembly line worker. Leonard was choosing to enter a career that my grandfather supervised and likely had little patience for.

Perhaps, though it was not spoken of much, my grandparents even secretly hoped that Leonard would not choose either a blue-collar or white-collar job at an automotive company but instead lean toward a white-collar vocation, the kind of white-collar that is partially covered by the black shirt of a priest, within the local Catholic diocese. In her later years, my grandmother often spoke of how she had always wanted a priest in the family, and the realization that her oldest son was not only not going to be a priest but was going to adopt a son and work as an hourly employee must have truly made her question, though she loved him deeply, his life choices and where she went wrong as a parent.

My mother's family, as blue-collar as a family can be, was very open and caring to me. There was no illusion that having me prevented my mother from achieving some grandiose dream. They accepted and loved me from the start. Though I never knew my mother's father, he died of a heart attack before I was born, his hard-driving blue-collar roots germinated into the seeds that blossomed into sons and daughters of the same ilk. My mom's sisters, my aunts, all worked hard raising families and working jobs that allowed them to earn money and raise children as well. My uncles all worked tirelessly on the assembly line at General Motors complaining about how they were treated by management and generally finding ways to escape the reality of their day-to-day jobs through chemical assistance, legal and otherwise.

In the late 1960s, after they were married, my mother and adoptive father bought a small home in the northwest end of Flint, Michigan. Though very small, roughly one thousand square feet., it was a place of their own in a community of other blue-collar factory workers who shared like-minded goals and aspirations. It was a racially diverse community with whites, blacks, Italians, and Polish, and it was a miniature melting pot of what America is often thought of.

My time in this community was the earliest of my formative years. From the time before I could walk to the years just before my adolescent teenage years, this was the community I called home. When I look back on that time, I think of walking a mile to school as a first grader through the city of Flint. I also recall walking a half mile to the drive-through liquor and cigarette shop, Sunshine Party store, and buying a pack of cigarettes and a beer for my dad for a dollar and having enough change to buy a piece of bazooka bubble gum as well. I look back in amazement at the innocence of the time that a seven-year-old could walk across the city of Flint, buy cigarettes and beer, and carry them back home without a question or concern. I contrast that to today's culture where I have to show my driver's license to purchase a can of spray paint or a bottle of cough medicine, and I wonder about the direction of our society. I contemplate what has changed so much that children of today have such a desperate need to escape reality that they will use anything they can find to alter their reality.

Primary Education

Though the idea of the one-room schoolhouse is not often thought of when discussing schooling in the downtrodden industrial city of Flint, Michigan, that was what I attended during this time. Each grade consisted of a small building, like a schoolhouse you see on an old western movie with one for each grade, kindergarten through third grade. The building on the far end of this photo was the kindergarten I attended, and the building nearest was third grade. I think, though to this day I am not sure, the bars were to keep criminals out and not for keeping students in. On the asphalt surrounding the schoolhouses was the playground—a swing set, a jungle gym, and of course, the deadly teeter-totter. We would run around on this playground on recess, jump off one end of the teeter-totter to let the other person smash to the ground—what a great joke that was—and generally burn off the energy that all children at this age possess.

I was blessed to be able to grasp the concepts of elementary education that were presented to me in those early years. So much so in fact that school became a bit boring for me at a young age. To pass the time, I would bring in a set of playing cards and teach the other children how to play rummy and Euchre. If you are from Michigan, learning to play Euchre is a mandatory rite of passage into adulthood. At my mother's family gatherings in Birch Run when I was young, I would sit at the side of the table and watch the adults play round after round of Euchre. I learned when to pass, when to pick it up, and when to play it alone. As I reflect on this, these decisions made in playing cards are synonymous with the decisions we make as adults every day. When do I pass on what seems a risky proposition, when do I take the cards dealt to me and go forward trying to beat the challenge of the day, and when am I so confident, when do I feel the cards dealt to me are so good that I can charge ahead on my own, with no assistance from others. Little did I know when I was a child, the card game being played before me would be a metaphor for life.

Regardless of the obvious, to me, philosophical and spiritual ramifications of playing cards, my second-grade teacher was less than impressed that I chose to spend my time in math teaching the finer parts of card games to fellow students instead of studying or putting my head down quietly and waiting for others to finish. A note was sent home to my mother informing her of my wanton disregard of adult direction.

This general idea of me knowing what was best for me also manifested itself in my behavior on the playground. I was sure that since I had already finished the afternoon's assignment, it would not benefit my long-term intellectual growth, as a second grader, to sit in class all afternoon with my head down. I developed a plan to escape recess and spend the afternoon hanging around the neighborhood. This plan, more intricately devised than any escape from Alcatraz, freed me from yet another afternoon of repeated lessons I already understood. As the bell rang to return to class, I had my friend feign injury to distract the recess aid while I quietly slipped away through the field and into the passage of my newfound freedom. It never occurred to me when devising my brilliant plan that my teacher apparently took a silent attendance after recess to make sure everyone that went out came back in. When that number was one short, a quick call from the school to my mother quickly thwarted my plans for a joyful spring afternoon. Not knowing where to go, I simply returned to my neighborhood when I had escaped class. I had not even comfortably settled in under the big tree down the road from my house when I heard my mom calling out my name. How was this possible? Who had ratted me out? It was not possible not to turn myself in because my mother finished her call out to me with, "If you don't come home now, you're going to be in even bigger trouble." As I popped my head out from under the tree I was hiding behind to see my mother standing on the steps of the house waiting for me, I felt like I understood the term "dead man walking." Slowly, step by reticent step, I trudged home to the belt I knew was waiting to embrace its familiar spot on my behind. Oh, that brief taste of freedom was sweet however and has been a goal of mine to achieve ever since.

Racial Harmony

Though this time of my life occurred shortly after the death of Dr. Martin Luther King, John and Bobby Kennedy, and the tumult of the Vietnam War, my memories of friendships and society at the time were reflected in the innocence of youth. I had friends of many colors and ethnicities. I guess when you are lower class, you don't have the opportunities to isolate yourself and your families into communities of those that look and think only like you. You play the hand of cards you are dealt, and you either live angry about your circumstances or you embrace the beauty of the people in your life. For me, for whatever reason, I was blessed to be able to choose the second option. My best friends where white and black, Catholic and Baptist, Polish, Italian, and whatever else that came from the mixing pot of our culture. To me, they were simply my friends. Though everyone's parents certainly must have been aware of the political and social climate of the time, the National Guard had been deployed to

put down riots just an hour south of our community; they did not seem to share this racial tension with their children that I played with nor into the houses where I was invited for dinner.

Simple fun, such as playing catch with a baseball, playing touch football, taking pony rides on the horse that was walked through the neighborhood, and jumping our bikes over ramps with our younger sisters as the objects we were jumping over were all fully integrated events. It never came to our mind to even consider anything different. When I got in playground or front yards fistfights with friends, I fought them because of some silly reason, but certainly not a racial reason. Always, if not later that afternoon, at the latest the next day, us young combatants would be back in the front yard playing as if nothing had ever happened.

Sadly, I think it was after one of my uncles had been stabbed on a bus in Flint by a black man that I first heard the term "nigger." I could tell by the hatred and anger in his voice that the term was not meant to be flattering, and I recall my mother telling me that I was never to say that word. I seem to also recall that my grandmother would listen to my uncle tell the story, cringe at the word, and then ask him not to say that word anymore in her house. Living in Flint and working in the factory, my father and my uncles lived and worked in an integrated environment every day. It was just the way it was, and I don't remember it being brought up as something to even think about.

Though it has been fifty years since Dr. King's nonviolent attempts at racial integration and harmony and his assassination at the Lorraine Hotel on April 4, 1968, I fear we are no further ahead in resolving the original sin of America than we were at the time of my childhood. It may simply be that the racist voices are the loudest in the crowds, and with today's need for information and a good 140-character storyline, they get the undeserved attention of the masses. It certainly does not appear that we have achieved the dreams of so many from that time of the civil rights movement.

It is without hesitation I say that one of the greatest gifts my parents gave to me was a lack of judgment of other based upon race. I am able to recognize that there are both brilliant and hateful people within every color, creed, religion, and ethnicity. I also think that living in communities where I was the minority pulled away the scales from my eyes and allowed me to both see and viscerally feel the truth and pain of what prejudice looks and feels like.

Altered States

The culture at the time of my early adolescence was one that had come to embrace breaking away from traditional rules and norms. With the social unrest of the Vietnam War, the throwing away of their parents' values at events such as Woodstock and the readily available supply of drugs, experimentation was openly accepted for my parents' generation. I saw this firsthand at a young age. Whether in family gatherings or when babysitting my younger cousins, watching some of the adults in my life use drugs was the norm. Smoking marijuana was just something my relatives did when they got together and not something that was considered radical or any different than smoking cigarettes. I came to accept it as just something the family did when we got together and didn't really give it much thought. On the rare occasions when one of my relatives must have come into a bit more money, they would partake in the harder variety of recreational drug use. Watching with keen interest as they would roll the opium into a little ball, stick it on the end of a pin that was pushed through a playing card, and trap the smoke with a juice glass seemed the most creative use of standard household items I had ever seen. Seeing that you really did snort cocaine by putting it on a mirror, split it into lines with a razor, and snort it into your nose through a rolled-up dollar bill made me feel like I was living a part of the *Miami Vice* television show that was very popular at the time.

To be clear, I only watched these things take place, and without hesitation, my relatives would tell me never to do this stuff myself. There was no crazy drug culture going on in the house, no dealers coming by, no drug deals going down in the driveway. I assumed they just picked up the drugs at work from coworkers who were somehow connected and brought them home and used them when they had someone responsible present, sometimes me, sometimes my grandmother. I never really saw my parents use these types of drugs in my presence. Their drug of choice was the legalized liquid form known as alcohol. In retrospect, I was never really clear why the stuff that you smoked or snorted was deemed by society to be illegal when the side effects I saw were a calming of the user and just a general relaxation.

Conversely, I would watch my parents partake in the commercialized, highly acceptable mind-altering drug known as liquor and get fall down drunk, angry at the world, and generally go into a condition I had no desire to enter myself or be around. The continuing hypocrisy of the American culture on what drugs are okay (alcohol, opioids, prescription narcotics) and which ones are illegal (marijuana) continues to leave me shaking my head. I do understand that if the government has no ability to tax it and generate income from it, then it is deemed not acceptable. Many people's acceptance without question of this hypocritical policy leaves me in amazement.

As I grew up, I still don't understand why I never had a desire to drink, smoke, or do drugs of any sort. It was certainly acceptable for a young man to experiment with drinking, have one of those bouts of drinking his dad's beer sort of moments. To me, someone who certainly wanted to escape the reality of their situation, this escape mechanism never appealed to me. As I grew much older, I recognized that one had to dig down to the root of one's issues to understand why there was even a need to drink, to escape. It is socially acceptable to say I'm just having a drink to loosen up, to unwind, but the question is, why is there such a lack of balance in our lives we need to unwind. Tools such as meditation and prayer provide an outlet to free one's mind, to unwind from the pressures of the everyday without escaping through alternative methods.

Maturing in a family where drug use was not seen as something out of the ordinary and was acceptable by all standards very much shaped the perspective I have to this day on the topic. I learned it was okay to question what society deemed as acceptable and ask why. Why is this illegal, why is this dangerous, who sets the rules we are asked to follow? Simply following without question the rules that are given to you or what society expects from you is far more dangerous than questioning, inquiring, seeking. Often times we learn to understand why some rules or norms are in place, and it brings tranquility to our questioning minds. I keep a wary eye on those around me who seem to follow without question, to accept direction without pausin wonder why. I think of societies of the not too distant past where the citizenry followed their elected leaders even though the direction was so clearly contrary to the common love and decency that should be accorded to all men. So, while I do not support drug usage of any sort as I feel it is crutch to working through one's real issues, I do not oppose it from a legalistic view based upon what the government leadership of the year tells the populace is acceptable and what is not.

Midwestern Roots

The idea that where one was raised helps to shape the basic set of core beliefs we have is both accurate and overly simplistic. There is no one Midwestern culture any more than there is one southern culture or one west coast culture. There may be major themes that unite those that live in a geographical area, but every person has their own specific adaptation to their culture. Growing up in the Midwest, particularly Michigan, in the seventies and eighties, I was immersed in a blue-collar manufacturing culture. Many of my family and friends either worked in a factory or on a farm. To this day, driving by a pasture after it has been freshly fertilized brings back very pleasant memories to me while often making those around me gag or plug their nose.

The area I grew up was famously labeled the Rust Belt. As a vehicle or any piece of machinery ages, the telltale sign of that age is rust along the edges of the equipment. Well, in the 1970s and 1980s, the rust was surely beginning to show along the edges of the Midwest. Foreign car companies began to take a firm hold of US automotive market share. The family farms began to become a thing of the past as large corporate farms took over that industry. The results of these changes in the basic way these industries functioned hit my hometown area especially hard. With a decrease in sales of automobiles from the big three (GM, Ford, Chrysler), fewer factories were required. The factories that were the first to be closed were the very old ones that had not incorporated any new technologies into them and were very expensive to operate. Many of these were in the Flint, Michigan, and surrounding areas. As the factories closed, the myriad of ancillary businesses that support these manufacturing behemoths also felt the brunt of modernization. When one factory that may directly employ four thousand employees closes, the entire community is affected. As you drive through communities like Flint, Michigan; Moraine, Ohio; or Janesville, Wisconsin, all vibrant communities at one time, it is easy to see the financial devastation that occurs when the major employer of the town shutters its doors. This was the environment that surrounded my formative childhood and teenage years.

Many of the people that worked in these factories that closed were forced to either take much lower-paying jobs or leave the state in search of other similar type of work across the nation. Many factory workers headed south to support the oil boom of the time. Many books and songs have been written of this great migration of the working class. To live in the center of it, to see the forced change of lifestyle that was required was an eye-opening experience for a young man looking to find a career choice at that time. I realized at an early age that there was no long-term career path for me as an hourly factory worker. I saw the frustration of this life lived out in the faces of my adopted father, uncles, and grandparents and knew the hourly shop life was not something I wanted to pursue. Certainly not because I was too good for that life, but because of the uncertainty I saw at the time and knowing I wanted a long-term career that would support my family. To this day, I have deep respect for those who get up each day and go to work in a factory to make a living to support their family. Contrary to the image that some TV shows and newspaper articles may paint, it is no longer a life of sitting in a chair or standing on a line reading the newspaper. Like all industries that have changed to survive, hourly factory workers work hard day in and day out doing a job that is often thankless.

For me, graduating high school at this time in history in the Midwest, I really had no idea what I wanted to do "when I grew up." I thought college was a good idea but had very little money and was not even sure what career path I would choose. I thought about a career in the military but had a serious girlfriend at the time and thought so little of myself that I was sure if I went off to the military,

I would lose my girlfriend, Lori, and surely never find another person to love me like she did. I knew I needed to work but was not really sure what I was equipped to do. I did get good grades in my high school drafting classes, and I very much liked the organization and planning that went into creating engineering drawings and layouts. In a life that was a bit chaotic due to divorce and addiction issues of those around me, the ability to organize and neatly layout engineering drawings was something that energized and intrigued me and was perhaps something I could do for a career. Basically, by default, and not really having a mentor or father to help guide me, I followed this path of employment opportunities to start my career.

CHAPTER 2
God Is Always Present

The smallest seed of faith is better than the largest fruit of happiness.
—Henry David Thoreau

Faith as a Youth

From my earliest age, my faith has always been an integral part of my life. On the day of my birth, God manifested His presence to my mother in a tangible way that I live with to this day. When I was born in Saginaw, Michigan, the only family members present were my mother (quite obviously) and my grandmother. When I had successfully entered into this world early on the morning of July 9, 1966, the doctor asked my mother if she had a name picked out for me, and she said yes, and instead of the name she had originally chosen, out came Martin Paul. For whatever reason, instead of the name she had picked out for me, out came the name of two local Catholic priests whom I would be forever named after. To this day, my mother still says she has no idea why these names came to her, but as my namesakes were Catholic priests that she knew and respected, she felt it was God's way of telling her that this was indeed to be my name. With no father present or a part of my life at the time of my birth, being named after two priests was tangible evidence to me that my real Father was not of this earth and would always be there for me regardless of the presence of those on earth.

I think often of the epidemic of fatherless children in the United States. It seems that since the sexual revolution of the 1960s, the increase in numbers of children born with no father figure in their life has risen exponentially. I believe this phenomenon cuts across racial lines while perhaps being more prevalent in some socioeconomic cultures than others. The children born into these situations, while definitely not doomed to failure, are certainly faced with a more difficult path than those children born into a household with both a mother and father figure.

When checking statistics from the US Census Bureau, the data there substantiates the general feeling of more single parent homes now. In 1970, four years after I was born, there were 3.4 million single family homes in the US with 3 million of those being single moms and 400,000 being single dads. In the 2000 census, that number had risen from 3.4 million single-parent homes to 12 million single-parent homes. In 2000, there were 10 million single-mother homes and 2 million single-father homes. I feel fervently that a strong family unit is the basis for a successful and happy childhood and a launching pad for success and happiness as an adult. Certainly one can be happy as a child and adult growing up in a single family home, but so much of the basis of how we understand our life comes from our parents, and when this is done as a partnership, the ability to see two sides of an issue and the importance of team work and compromise is visible.

Religious Influences

From the time I was young, I always recall the presence of a priest or a nun or a religious person in my life. There has been much publicity about scandals with religious leaders across denominations and the children that are entrusted to them. Like the majority of children who are active in the church, I never witnessed or experienced any hint of improper behavior. I was often left alone with people from the church, both religious and laity, those who are not ordained, and never experienced anything but caring people willing to take their own time to share their faith.

My earliest memories of direct interaction with a priest are from when I was likely no more than five or six years old. My father's family was Polish Catholic and very active in their faith. It was not uncommon back in the late sixties and early seventies, directly after Vatican II, a landmark change in the Catholic church, for families to invite clergy to their house for dinner. Living in the Detroit area near Hamtramck, a bastion of Polish immigrants in Michigan, my great-grandparents were part of a larger Catholic community. It was not uncommon at that time for families to get together every Sunday or for special occasions like birthdays and anniversaries. I assume that because my father's family were first and second generation immigrants from Poland, the family may have been especially close due to the nature of immigrants and the sense of camaraderie and community that the family felt.

On a particular family get-together, there was a young priest that was invited over for the family dinner. In retrospect, I believe it may have been a young seminarian. These seminarians are young men, often in their early twenties, who are discerning priestly vocations. They often live at the seminary away from their families, and the opportunity to join a parish family for a homemade meal and family time away from their studies are indeed cherished opportunities. I suspect now with the advent of mobile communication technology and apps like Skype, it is easy to keep in touch with family and perhaps less of that longing for family is present.

During this get-together in my early years, I remember vividly sitting on the back porch and talking to the seminarian for what seemed to me like hours. I had never seen a person in a priestly collar so young. I had also never seen a seminarian or priest outside of the church. To see a young, vibrant seminarian in his priestly black shirt and pants, sitting at my family's house, eating and drinking with the rest of us was a powerful experience for me. I remember, though it was likely forty-five years ago, being incredibly curious about what the faith life of a priest was and asking this seminarian endless questions to which I recall him patiently answering. In retrospect, he may have been as intrigued with me as I was of him. Regardless, it was my first experience as seeing priests as human beings, just regular people, trying to live their lives in the best way they knew how to serve God. I often wonder who that seminarian was; he would be about seventy years old now. Did he complete his discernment and follow the path of priesthood or did his life take him in another direction?

As the years ground by at an unbelievably slow pace, as it does for all children who want to grow up and do things, I was never far from my faith. Though not living a particularly active faith life growing up, I attended catechism every week during the school year and mass every Sunday. Catechism is the weekly classes that young catholic children are required to attend to receive the sacraments. So, prior to first communion where we receive the body and blood of Jesus Christ, reconciliation (or confession), and confirmation, students learn about the scriptural basis for these sacraments and are prepared to better understand the meaning of them. I can't say I especially enjoyed attending these classes. Often the same kids that I didn't get along with at the public schools I attended were fellow Catholics and attended these classes as well.

I recall walking home from town one day. I believe I must have been in fifth or sixth grade. I may have been walking back from the party store during summer vacation as I remember it was warm and it was a weekday. It is indicative of the change in culture as I can't imagine I would have left my sons walk a couple of miles up town when they were nine or ten years old.

On the way home, my route took me past the local Catholic church I attended at the time, St. Rita in Holly, Michigan. The old stone church is still there today. As I walked past it, I remember vividly that I had a strong desire to go inside and pray. I went to the doors to go in, and they were locked. I couldn't believe the church, the house of God, was locked. All I wanted to do was go inside and sit in a pew and pray. So, not being able to enter, I did the next best thing and kneeled down on the concrete steps outside the church and prayed there. I vaguely recall my friend I was walking with wondering what in the world I was doing, and I imagine he was wondering how long I would be. Throughout my life, regardless of the choices I had made and my proximity to God, I have always felt Him near to me.

I assume like most children who attend church, I recall sitting in the pews wondering what the priest was talking about and why it seemed so boring. I will say that homiletics, the gift of being able to give an engaging, educational, and spirit-filled homily or sermon, has not always been the strength of the priests at the churches I have attended. While I truly recognize that it is a gift of the Holy Spirit to be able to communicate His message in a way that grabs the people in the pews and draws them in, there must have been a severe lack of homiletics training for many years. I think I really wanted to be engaged, but often the sermons seemed so off topic or, sadly, boring, I simply could not get interested even though I tried mightily. I was glad to see that the Archdiocese of Detroit seems to have recognized this issue as well and had a fine homiletics teacher at the seminary I attended. While I love the sacraments and the history that that Catholic church has to offer, I have often found better sermons delivered in Pentecostal or other Christian churches. I have been blessed in recent years to have seen what seems to be a change in this however and have seen many amazing young priests deliver powerful, spirit-filled sermons that draw in the faithful and touch them at a very deep level.

CHAPTER 3
Fatherhood

His leaving wasn't about you; it was about him.
—Iyanla Vanzant

Where Are You, Dad?

I don't recall at what age I found out that my dad, the man that I saw each day when I came home from school, was not the man that was there when I was created. I would have thought that finding out that whom you thought was your father was not your biological father would have been a significant moment in my life, but to this day, I cannot remember the day I found out. It was like I just always knew that he and his side of the family were not my "real" family. Now, this is not to suggest they did not love me or treat me like one of the family; they did, but there was always just something a little different.

I do recall my mother asking me at a young age if I wanted to know anything about my biological father, my "real dad." At that point, I kind of felt like he had already left me once, so I didn't need or want to know anything about him. I do think back and wonder if I wanted to know but was too proud or wanted to show I didn't need him to get through this life, but I honestly do not recall feeling any desire to have any information about him. In retrospect, having recently found out who my biological father was through the science that is now available through the DNA tracking programs that are available, I wish I would have found out sooner as finding out that I have another brother and sister near my age would have been nice to know earlier in my life, but more on that later.

Growing up in my family, I often felt just a little less a part of the family than everyone else. My mother and adopted father had two daughters that were younger than me. So, as I grew up, I kind of felt like I wasn't fully a part of the team. I don't think I was treated that differently from my siblings, but every now and then, I would hear someone say something like, "Well that's not his real dad," or "Those are only his half-sisters," and I would be reminded of the reality of the situation. To be clear, though we grew up on the lower end of the spectrum financially, I was blessed to have a large contingent of grandparents, aunts and uncles, and others that surrounded us. I had a roof over my head, though for many years it was a double-wide trailer, and food to eat, though often it was provided by the government in the form of a block of hard yellow material often referred to as "government cheese." I will still say, to this day, that welfare cheese warmed up in the microwave between two slices of Wonder Bread is one of the go-to meals of my life.

This socioeconomic status I was raised in helped form my view on many things as I got older. I cringe when I hear the term "trailer trash" as that is the housing I grew up in. I shake my head when I hear people who have never had to wonder about what they would eat for their next meal talk about ungrateful welfare recipients and what a bunch of freeloaders anyone on welfare is. I have come to realize that any term that generalizes a group of people based upon their color, their housing situation, their faith, their economic status is always, always incorrect. I have been blessed to experience overwhelming grace and beauty from people of every age, color, religion, and nationality. Some of the kindest and most giving people I have met have been those who have the least financial means to give. Some of the most cruel and bigoted people I have met have been those who have been blessed with privilege and material items their entire life.

Having money, being a certain color, or having a specific faith does not mean that we will be kind or caring. All humans have a capacity for love and sacrifice for others just as all humans have a capacity for hatred and emotional and spiritual ugliness. It is the choices we make when that still, small voice in the back of our head whispers to us. When we hear that voice that says, "It's wrong to make fun of that person for how they look," "You should stand up for that person who is being bullied," "You should not go along with your peers doing something you know to be wrong," it is how we respond during these times, whether we listen to that voice and not the other factors of race, religion, and color, that defines who we are.

Adrift into Manhood

My parents' divorce happened in the years just prior to me becoming a teenager. I am vague about it because I do not recall the exact age that my adopted father and my mother divorced. The divorce was a theatrically bitter divorce between two people who could no longer seem to be in the same room together let alone making the journey through life hand in hand. There were drunken arguments that ended in physical violence; there were things said to us children by both parents that no child should ever have to hear about their parents, and there was raging anger and hatred flowing through the house just as tangible and sure as the electricity that powered the lights.

I recall being told by my adopted father that he wouldn't be seeing me anymore because he had a new family now and he had to take care of them. I assume, maybe incorrectly, that this message was also shared with my younger sisters. I imagine how painful it may have been to them, how difficult it was to process as this was their real father. For me, it led to a lifetime of feelings of being an inadequate son. By the time I was thirteen or so, my biological father and my adopted father had viscerally chosen not to have me in their life. It's only now after many years of reflection, counseling, and prayer that I recognize those choices that seemed to me at the time to be a reflection of me had nothing to do with me personally but instead were the choices of men who for various reasons did not feel they could be in the situation to be a parent to my siblings and me nor in a relationship with my mother. Like a soldier who is injured by shrapnel meant to destroy the enemy, so often children of divorce are emotional causalities of this friendly fire. Children are caught in this crossfire of hatred and anger and are left to deal with the unseen wounds for the rest of their life.

As my adopted father left the mobile home to us, my mother, my two younger sisters, and my grandmother and me, I was subjected to the dreaded phrase you never want to hear as a very young man, "You are the man of the house now." How to process that as a twelve- or thirteen-year-old boy? What does that mean? What does that look like from a functional perspective? Are my sisters supposed to listen to me like I am their father, because that didn't seem to be happening. Was I not supposed to go and play with other guys my age? Because certainly men don't play; they take care of their family by working and raising money. I think I was told I was the man of the family as a way of saying, "Don't worry. We don't need your father. Between us, we will make this work," but I don't feel this is how it was interpreted by a young man who had seen two fathers distance themselves from him before he was even a teenager.

With all this written about this time in my life, I will say that I was actually very blessed. I was never subject to any form of abuse, other than a few belts across my backside that, if I'm honest, I very much deserved. I never went to bed too hungry. I had presents to open on Christmas, even if they were donated by fellow church members. I have seen much in my travels around the world and have seen many people, children, and adults that do not have access to all the things I did as a child—warm, clean, safe running water, clothes to wear, and a roof over their heads. I was also always taken to church to grow in my faith and had the luxury of questioning God. The internal comfort it provides knowing that there is a creator who loved me and listened to me sustained me through many difficult times.

An Unknown Gift

My biological father, though I never met him, unknowingly left me a great gift through his personal choices. As I reached my fiftieth birthday, I had started to reach out though a genealogy service to recreate my family tree. I had filled in many of the branches on my mother's side, but one side of the tree was very bare—no branches or leaves to illustrate the beauty of God's creation. As I started to get older, I was often asked by physicians during the mandatory yearly physicals my job required if I had any family background of specific diseases or illnesses. I was told I wouldn't need to check for colon cancer unless there was a history of it in my family. Of course, I could only provide half the story as I was not even sure who my dad was, let alone if him or his family had any history of illnesses. So, using this as justification, allowing me to research without admitting I was curious to learn of my family history for other reasons, I sent in a DNA sample to see if I could find out more about my family lineage.

The DNA results took several weeks, but when they arrived, I was greatly surprised at the results. Instead of my family history being primarily western Europe, France, England, and such, I was primarily of Scandinavian descent. While this was interesting and a fun fact to know, I suddenly felt closely linked to the Vikings and Norse legends; it brought me no closer to understanding my family history.

The genealogy service that I subscribed to gives me e-mail notifications when potential new family members are identified. Often they are fifth cousins of an in-law's stepmothers' brother or some other obscure connection. Early in 2017, I received a notification of a possible first cousin or sibling. Since I felt confident I knew all my siblings and first cousins, I assumed that perhaps this was someone from my father's side of the family. After doing a little research on the person who was identified, I was quickly able to ascertain by her last name, which was the same as my father's, that this person was in fact my sister. How to reach out, if to reach out, when to reach out all became questions for me. I could not assume that this person even knew that they had a brother or sister they were not aware of. After much prayer and contemplation, I sent a brief e-mail though the genealogy service identifying that we had been potentially listed as siblings and if we could talk. My sister, likely not knowing who in the world I was, did not respond immediately. In fact, she forwarded my note to her, our, brother to reach out to me.

I received a text message from my brother asking who I was and what this was about. I replied suggesting that it would be better for us to talk instead of discussing this via text.

After setting up a time to talk, I became a little nervous. How would I tell my brother who I was and that his dad had children that he had not reached out to and that they likely did not even know about? When my brother answered the phone, I just sort of got straight to the point. After listening for a bit, my brother shared some information about himself and our dad. He gave me a short Wikipedia version of my family history. It was enlightening and a bit overpowering at the same time. I wish I had thought to have a pencil and paper available to take notes. There was so much information about my dad, his parents, my siblings, my niece and nephews, etc. Wow, so much to take in; it was a very powerful phone call.

I also found out during that call that my father had just recently passed away, and I would not be meeting him anytime soon. My father seemed to have a penchant for fast cars, and late the year prior to the phone call with my brother, he had crashed his sports car along the side of the road. My brother sent pictures of the car as well as pictures of my father and grandfather from years before. I briefly lamented the passing of my father prior to meeting him in person. I wonder what reasons there were for me to find out about him after fifty years on this earth only to get the information a few months after he passed. It seems as if it was not in God's plan for me to meet with my father on this earth. Also, perhaps my own stubbornness to admit that I was at all interested in knowing about the man whose genes I carry forward led to this delay in finding out about him. Regardless, the gift he gave me of a new brother and sister after so many years on this earth is something I am very grateful for.

As I learned more about my father, I was astounded at the proximity the arcs of our lives took toward each other. I had been told by my mother that my real father likely lived in California and his name was Gerald. When I did do some halfhearted Internet searches, I would search his last name and for Gerald in California. Little did I know he went by Jerry, and he actually had lived the majority of his life no more than twenty miles from where I had lived and raised my children.

As my wife shared my story with her friends, odd coincidences continued to manifest themselves. After sharing my story with a dear friend of hers, my wife told me that twenty-five years ago, my father had sponsored her friend's husband through Alcoholic Anonymous and that they had become family friends. My wife's friend, shaking her head in amazement, immediately saw the physical resemblance between my father and me and wondered how she had never put two and two together.

My father had owned a business in the same type of industry that I had built my career in. While I had worked in building machinery and equipment for automotive companies, my father had owned a steel construction company that supplied material to the industry that I worked in. Every day as I talked to the newfound gifts of my brother and sister and their family, I found more and more points of connection.

Upon reflection, I hold no ill will toward my father for the choices he made. When he decided to leave my mother to be with his wife at the time and father a son who would end up being but four months younger than me, he was making decisions as a result of choices he made as a teenager. I can only guess that as he never met or knew me, it made it easier for him to never want to inquire about how I was doing. Had he also fathered other children outside of wedlock in his younger years? Did he indeed wonder about me, but were shame and guilt a factor in never reaching out? Those are questions that only he can answer and that he had to live with throughout his life. As I see pictures of him as a father and grandfather and the joy he seemed to share with his grandchildren, I am happy to see that he seemed to have gotten to a good place in his life. I continue to cultivate the relationship between my newfound siblings and reach out to learn more about them as well as myself. Life is an amazing journey of discoveries, and if we open ourselves up with a loving heart, we can find joy, love, and amazing points of light along the way.

CHAPTER 4
A Child of Divorce

Divorce is an expensive punishment love gets when it fails.
—Bangambiki Habyarimana

Not Fitting In

Divorce is a relationship epidemic that has swept through the United States of America. It's no secret that the probability of having a marriage survive for the duration of the child's first eighteen years continues to plummet at an alarming rate. Though it stabilized a bit in the 1980s, divorce is still a plague on marital relationships to this day. In the 1950s and early 1960s when the parents of our generation were being raised as children, there was a 75 percent chance that their parents would remain married for the duration of their lives, a 75 percent chance that children would have only one or a maximum of two Christmas parties to attend each year, and only a 25 percent chance that children would have to integrate stepparents and stepbrothers and stepsisters into their lives. Current data suggests that between 40 percent to 50 percent of marriages now end up in divorce.

Growing up, I was part of a family that helped fuel the upward trend of marriages ending in divorce. While some divorces, over time, are actually amicable, the one I was involved with as a child was certainly not.

The ramifications of the divorce and the resultant reduced income into our household of residence seemed to set me even further apart from the other children I went to school with. Growing up in Flint, I was already a bit of an outsider when we moved into the small-town community of Holly, Michigan. I wore my hair long, my pants were plaid, and my clothes were hand-me-downs. To this day, I can recall the stigma of not fitting into the community I had moved into and being ashamed of the clothes I had. Our family was very firmly entrenched in the lower-class income levels. What money we did get went to purchase groceries, pay the rent, and cover the essentials. I quickly found out that things like new clothes, haircuts, birthday presents were not essential to us getting by.

I reflect now on how cruel children can be toward one another at that age, and truthfully at any age. I don't think this desire to make fun of others and criticize others is an inborn trait for a child. Instead, I believe that children hear others around them, their family, the parents, their peers, make fun of others, and children pick this up as a way to talk to and deal with others. While I certainly did not enjoy being made fun of by others, I did partake in that same behavior myself. In retrospect, it seemed like making fun of others allowed me to fit in with someone. I did not have enough internal confidence or pride in myself to stand up and say, "Stop, it is not okay to call someone a name because they are different." Instead, if going along with the joke at someone else's expense allowed me not to be the target and allowed me to fit in with that group, I sadly participated in the name-calling.

I do realize that all children growing up go through some sort of period where they don't fit in or where they struggle with their own identity. I wondered as a child what it would be like to grow up like many of my friends who had houses, not trailers, to grow up in. What would it be like to have had both a mom and dad home at night? What would a family dinner be like where the parents and children sat around the table and talked? I recognize that the idealistic family I witnessed when I visited friends' houses likely had their own issues, but to me, I saw a situation that I did not have and that I longed for.

My experience growing up with the assistance of the government through ADC, aid to dependent children, shapes me to this day. When I hear the typical campaign rhetoric of needing to get people off welfare because they are all lazy and collect the hardworking people's tax money, I simply shake my head and wonder if the people who make these statements have ever been down on their luck or taken assistance from others. Being on welfare was a humbling experience for me and I am sure for my mother. Getting Christmas presents donated to us because we could not afford to buy our own was never something we were proud of. I know that when our family was receiving welfare checks, food stamps, government cheese, we were all working very hard at a low-paying job trying to work toward a better life. To say all people who get welfare are lazy and are on drugs is so overly simplistic and simply not correct. It is no more accurate to suggest that than it is to say everyone on welfare just had a bad break. Whenever we paint an entire group with the same broad-brush strokes, we are sure to make mistakes.

Gender Roles

After my parents had divorced, I was the sole male inhabitant of a home that had a mother, a grandmother, and two younger sisters. Growing up in a home full of women certainly shaped who I am today. The traditional gender specific roles of a man and women were not evident in my house of origin. If dishes needed to be done, they were as much my responsibility as they were my sisters'. If laundry needed to be washed, I was as able to load clothes into the washer and dryer as well as my mother and sisters were. I certainly looked for a physical reason, some genetic specific restriction that would prevent me from doing these traditional female tasks but, alas, was unable to find a reason why a male could not do all these tasks as simply as a woman could. If I was hungry, I learned that cooking meals was a good way to help alleviate the hunger in my stomach.

I believe that learning at a young age how to iron, do dishes, wash clothes, and cook meals has served me well as an adult and as a husband. It did not, as my adoptive father told me to my face it would, make me into a homosexual because I grew up with all women and was doing "women's work." Instead, it helped me to eventually be able to show my sons the value of being able to take care of oneself by learning how to do these things.

I think that many of the tasks would have in fact been done by my mom if she had been home. But the fact that she went to school to get her degree and then took on a full-time job simply did not leave her time to do many of these chores. So, the work that traditionally a stay-at-home mom might do was often left to my sisters and me as well as my grandmother.

I will say that while I did help with all the chores around the house, I do not specifically remember my mom or sisters doing things like mowing the lawn. Perhaps they did help with that, but it seemed like the majority of "man's jobs" outside the house were left to me. I think that my need for organization also pushed me to take on some of this traditional man type work. I cannot stand it to this day if someone mows the lawn and does not do it in straight lines or does it haphazardly. I like the neatness of a freshly cut lawn with the straight lines and neat edges. I seem to recall my sisters and mother at that time and my wife to this day do not see the need for such precision when cutting a lawn.

So, in addition to seeing how it was possible and in fact helpful for a man to take on the traditional tasks that had been historically been done by a stay-at-home mom, I also saw the strength of an inspired and loving grandmother. My grandmother, Geraldine, lived with us for a several years to help my mother raise us when my mother was off at school or work. My grandmother was a loving and strong woman whom I believe I inherited much of what is good in me from.

Geraldine was strong and firm in her direction to us but at the same time loving and tender. If something had to be done, she would figure out a way to get it done. Born in the first part of the twentieth century, Geraldine grew up on a farm with no electricity and no running water. She raised six children in a small cinder block garage no larger than a modern two-car garage after Grandpa Carl had died at a relatively young age.

Her strength may have been fortified on October 4, 1956, when her oldest son, Dick, at the age of fourteen, was killed in an auto accident. Walking home from church, Dick was hit by a drunk driver. Though Geraldine was forty-three years old at the time, five children remained living at home at that time, desperately needing her care and direction.

It was not more than seven years later, on March 21, 1963, when her husband of twenty-nine years, Grandpa Carl, passed away from a heart attack. It was a normal Thursday afternoon, and Grandpa, who worked the afternoon shift, had not gotten up for work. A hardworking, hard-drinking union man who participated in the early labor movement for the UAW as they struggled to gain a foothold in the factories run by the automotive companies in the area, Carl worked and played hard. Knowing he was going to be late for work, Grandma had her son, my uncle, Lynn, go in to wake up his father for work. As hard as Lynn shook his father to wake him, he would not respond. Grandma came into the room to hear Lynn's pleas for his father to wake up to find her husband had died in his sleep. She was left to bury her husband and to raise five children, age ten to twenty-one on her own.

Prior to Grandpa dying, he had built a house for Grandma and the kids near the garage. The house must have seemed absolutely palatial to the family. It had indoor plumbing, electricity, and gas heat, all things that no one in the family had experienced when they were living in the brick garage.

Living on a farm in Birch Run, Michigan, when Grandpa passed, Grandma had access to food to feed her children. She was not reliant on welfare and food stamps to get food from the store. This was not the case when my mother and adopted father divorced in 1978.

Living in a mobile home with no real source of income, no garden to grow food, we were forced to rely on welfare to put food on our table. Being twelve years old at that time, I didn't really fully grasp the difference between paying for groceries with white paper stamps from a book as opposed to paying for them with green paper from a purse. It wasn't until I had to take groceries of the checkout belt and put them back on the shelf because we didn't have enough of the white paper stamps did I realize that there was something different in how we purchased groceries than many of my friends when I went with them.

Driving Mrs. Thrasher

Like many other children of divorce, the traditional roles of parents, the focus on work instead of school and the impact of other parental figures played a key role in my life.

One of my fondest memories with my grandma at this time was driving across several states to visit my aunt, her daughter, in Wisconsin. Since my grandmother had never owned or driven a car until she was in her fifties, after her husband had died and she needed to be able to get around on her own, she was never fond of driving. So, during one summer in the late 1970s, she asked me if I would like to visit my cousins in Wisconsin, on the other side of Lake Michigan. She also said, if I were to go, I could drive her car, a new Chevy Chevette during the trip. Being thirteen years old at that time, the idea of driving on my own across what seemed like the entire country seemed like an adventure I could not possibly pass up. So, we headed off on a warm July morning. Though I was thirteen at that time, I was likely as tall as my grandmother. The Chevette was a very small car, so it was easy, even for someone just freshly graduated from elementary school, to drive.

As one would expect, having never really driven before, driving for the first time on a cross-country trip had its share of adventures. It was pretty straightforward on the backcountry roads, but when I drove through larger towns like Flint and Green Bay, I went through my own accelerated driver's education class, in real time. Luckily there were no incidents during the adventure, but as I look back on this experience, I wonder if this is where my love for driving across the country originated from. Needless to say, when I eventually did have to take a real driver's education course when I turned sixteen, the course work and the driving test was pretty straightforward for me as I had already been driving for three years at that point. Apparently, the Chevy Chevette must have seemed like a very low-risk car to police drivers as I was never pulled over or questioned while driving.

I think these adventures while I was just a young teen also helped me to escape from the reality of my homelife at the time. While in Wisconsin, I was free to hang out with my three male cousins who had a somewhat more stable house with both their mother and father present. Having three sons in the house, the household in Wisconsin was a testosterone-driven domicile much in contrast to the house I lived with my sisters, my mother, and my grandmother. In Wisconsin, there was always someone for me to play catch with (instead of the side of the wall I would throw my tennis and baseballs against in Michigan), someone to walk to the park with to meet girls, and someone to listen to the latest rock albums with. It was a blissful escape for a few weeks each summer. The trip home was a dose of reality in which I understood that the reality of my existence would always come back into play.

Living in the Eye of the Storm

While traveling during the summer allowed me to escape the storm of my homelife, at the end of the day, it was always back into the maelstrom that we had to endure. There would be times of calm, inside the eye of the storm, but you knew that having just passed through the driving winds of rage and anger, the eye of the storm would pass, and again you would be buffeted by driving insults, cutting comments, and a general storm of anger and confusion.

Some of the most difficult times I can recall were when I would have my new friends over to the house for a visit. Just moving into Holly from Flint, I was at that transitional time where one is making new friends and establishing relationships with peers that would likely, without thinking about it at the time, define the groups I would spend time with and who would shape my life as I entered adolescence.

One of my closest friends when I moved to Holly near the end of elementary school was a very nice young man who had a really kind and caring family. His parents were teachers, and he had brothers and sisters who seemed to be very happy. When I would visit their house, they would have nice dinners, sit around the table, and share the day's adventures and generally not throw things at each other and let each other know what terrible individuals they were. It was quite a contrast to my home.

As I developed my friendship with this young man, he asked to come over to my house to visit and see where I lived. Apprehensive at first, I acquiesced, and he came home from school with me one day. When I arrived home from school, it was the time my dad would have been going into work, I guess, as he was home but only for a very short time. On this day, I assume that both him and my mother had been drinking as a tremendous fight broke out after I had arrived home. While the presence of alcohol was not required for my parents to fight, it was certainly the proverbial fuel on the fire, and the sparks that were always present in their relationship by this point would ignite into a rage-induced fire when either or both had been drinking. This particular fight escalated into a physical altercation with my mother hitting my father with some sort of cooking utensil; it may have been a cast iron pan, you know, the big, heavy black pans that weigh almost as much as a sledgehammer and pack an equal wallop. Neither parent being a pacifist, one sleight or physical attack would not go unanswered, so within moments of hitting him or at least threatening to, my mother was screaming to get out of the house as my father was going to kill her and us.

The wide-eyed look of terror and confusion on my friend's face was something I recall to this day. This sort of behavior was something he may have seen on television at this house, even that was unlikely based upon shows like *Happy Days* and *All in the Family* being the most popular at that time, but certainly not something he had been personally witness to. I recall after running out of the house and making sure everyone was okay, we left the yard to let things settle down. After a few minutes, I was able to get back into the house, and my friend called his mom to come pick him up for an emergency evacuation. This was prior to cell phones, so there were no video uploads of this event to social media and no way for my friend to reach his parents without getting back into the house to call from the landline.

His mother was in our driveway in less than five minutes, from the other side of town, and not surprisingly, it was the very last time that my friend ever visited my house.

Forty years later, I look back on this event and still cringe a bit. I was so very embarrassed that my parents had behaved this way in front of my friend and couldn't understand why they had to act this way. After becoming an adult and entering into a long-term marriage, I understand the cyclical ups and downs in a new relationship. I think I held these types of events against my parents for a long time but now understand them to be the results of two people struggling with their own issues and not having the proper tools to deal with emotions that were present. I said to myself at that time if I ever got married, I would never act this way and embarrass my kids in front of their peers. Not sure if I was able to completely honor that promise I made to myself, but it was always something I had set for myself as a parenting goal.

Work as an Escape

Several years after my parents had divorced, the tension in our household was still present. Family roles were not really understood, there was anger at our situation, and our relationships were enmeshed with each other. There was an underlying love for each other, I guess, but it was buried so deep under layers of anger, tension, hurt that it never really surfaced. As soon as I was able to, just before my sixteenth birthday, I got a job to escape the situation I lived in.

As I have learned throughout my life, it is really relationships that matter in all things. For me, my first experience with this was my first job. My mother worked for an attorney at that time as a legal secretary, and that attorney was friends with the owner of a local gas station. The gas station was looking for someone to work there in the afternoons, and I was looking to not be home in the afternoons and to make some money, so it was a perfect situation.

This first job of mine was in 1982, back when gas stations were still full service and people enjoyed not getting out of their car and having someone pump their gas for them. It was a pretty straightforward job. Someone pulls in, they tell you how much gas they want, and you in turn pump that much into their vehicle. After that, collect the money, and transaction complete. Part of it being a full-service station was that we also washed the windshields and checked the oil and tires as well.

It was a good job for me as it allowed me to work almost as many hours as I wanted, which was a lot, and allowed for a lot of room for additional responsibility. Within a few months, when I was still sixteen years old, I was responsible for closing the station at night, gathering the money, making a deposit slip, and depositing the day's money, often several thousand dollars, at the bank down the road. A few months later, and I was promoted, with no raise in pay, to manager and helped with scheduling, coordinating new hires, training new hires, and the list continued to grow.

While this was exciting and rewarding to me to be recognized, something I have craved my entire life, it also proved difficult at times. The staff at the gas station, as you can imagine, was a collection of guys from all walks of life and all ages, some looking to just get started, some down on their luck, and others who just needed a job. When the owner hired a midforties gentlemen who rode to work on his first day on his Harley and found out that I, a seventeen-year-old high school kid, was his boss, he was less than impressed. When I proceeded to tell this new hire that when it was slow, he had to paint curbs and clean up around the station, his response to me was, "I wasn't hired by you, and my job is only to pump gas." I told him that he would have to do the other items around the shop if he wanted to stay. As he continued to refuse to see the importance of this busy work as I did, I had to call the owner and let him know of the situation. The owner advised me that, as manager, I would have to fire this biker dude with tattoos and who knows what else in the saddlebags of his Harley. I slowly, believe me very slowly, walked up to him and advised him I was firing him because he just wasn't working out. He quite plainly told me I couldn't fire him, and he was going to kick my ass. It was at this point that my sense of humor, which has been misunderstood for the greater part of my life, exerted itself, and I told this guy that fine, I couldn't make him leave, but I could only ensure he wouldn't get paid for staying on. "Feel free to stay and work. You just won't be getting paid for it." For whatever reason, he did not find this as funny as I thought it was, and I could tell it took a lot of restraint on his part not to fulfill his promise to kick my ass. In retrospect, I think it was a good thing I was still a minor as it may have saved me from a good beating.

I stayed with this job for several years and took on more and more responsibility though the pay never really increased. I started at $3.35 an hour and eventually worked my way all the way to nearly $4.00 an hour. It was a good first job as I got to take on a lot of responsibility, to meet many people in the community, which would come to help me later, and it put a few dollars in my pocket.

By this time, I had met Lori, my first real girlfriend, who would eventually become my first wife, more on that later, and the money was helpful for new clothes, haircuts, gas, and everything else I needed but my mother was unable to provide based upon the money she made.

The job and the money quickly became much more important to me than school or many other activities that a high schooler should be concerned about. After about three months working at the station, my schedule bumped up to about forty hours a week. I think laws somewhat prohibit this now, but at that time, there were not really any restrictions, and I liked the money and being away from home. I would start school around 7:00 a.m., when I went, which was pretty infrequently, and get out around 2:00 p.m. By 2:30 p.m., I would be at work and work until 10:30 p.m. I would work this schedule four days during the week and would then usually work a weekend day as well. There were times, actually most of the time, I was so tired, and I would look ahead several days to see when I would be able to get any sleep or do any homework. I just remember my junior and senior year always being tired and always just trying to get by. By the time high school ended, it was such a tremendous relief for me not to have to spend time in school any longer, and I could finally find time for other things that I felt school had held me back from for so long. Fortunately that same work ethic, which I think I picked up from my mother and grandmother, has helped me throughout my career as I went into more corporate-type jobs.

First Experience With Racism

During my time working at the gas station, I had my first real experience with racism. I had of course heard, read, and studied about racism through school and through reading the stories in the paper. It seemed far away though and not something that I really felt was local and real.

As I was a pretty reliable worker, my boss asked me if I had any friends that might want a job as well. If they worked as hard as me, he would be happy to hire them. It did not occur to me that this offer came with any caveats or restrictions.

I asked Steve, one of my best friends, who was looking for a job if he would be interested. My friend was honest, funny, and a hard worker, and I thought would be someone I would enjoy working with, and with his outgoing and funny personality, he would do great at the station. I arranged for an interview with the owner and my friend one cool spring day and was excited to have a friend working at the station, someone I could ride to work with, share stories, etc.

My friend Steve had his interview, and as he was walking out, I asked him how it went, expecting he would be starting the next day or so. He told me that there was not enough work right now to justify hiring someone but that the owner told him he would keep his name on file. This was pretty confusing to me as I saw how much work there was, saw the openings in the staffing schedule, and knew that there was a spot available.

Shortly after Steve left, my boss asked me to come into his office. I could tell he was a bit uncomfortable. "Marty," he said, "I can't hire your friend." I thought Steve must have really said something wrong or did something to upset the owner. "Marty, he is black, and I can't hire a black guy to work for me in this town." I couldn't believe what I was hearing. He really wasn't going to hire my friend because the color of his skin. Nothing about he wasn't qualified, he was a smart aleck. Nothing, just simply, "I can't hire him because he is black." There were a number of older customers, older white men, who did not want a black guy working in their town. I had thought all the old customers that came in were great guys, and they had always treated me well and even tipped me at times. After hearing this, I found myself trying to figure out which of the customers were racist and who would have had such a strong influence on my boss to sway his decision on whom to hire. Looking back, I wonder if it was not my boss himself who had the racial issues and used "the customers" as an excuse not to hire my friend.

It was at that moment that I realized that the racism I heard about on TV and studied about in school was a real and tangible thing. My friend told me the next day he knew he was not going to get the job as soon as he walked in and met my boss. I was embarrassed that I had asked him to come in an interview and that he had to deal with that. His response? "No big deal, it happens all the time." That shocked me even more. To me, that was an eye-opening experience; to my friend, it was just part of growing up black in a primarily white town.

CHAPTER 5
Married Life

*My most brilliant achievement was my ability to
be able to persuade my love to marry me.*

—Sir Winston Churchill

Marrying Young

Having generally survived my childhood adventures, I began to grow, learn, and develop more adult relationships. When I was sixteen, having never really had a serious girlfriend before, I met my future wife. Due to the tumultuous relationships and atmosphere in my house, I spent a lot of time at friends' houses. Though their houses may not have been the model of the nuclear family, they were friendly, and issues there were not my issues to deal with. I could hang out and play games and read comic books and not have to deal with the drama at my house.

One of my best friends at that time was a classmate named Kevin who was in my grade in high school. I would often stay at his house on weekends, and we would go to comic book stores and read comics. All the Marvel action movies that are so popular now were rooted in the comic book generation that grew up during the seventies and eighties.

Fortunately for me, Kevin had a sister who was two years younger than him. His sister was very nice; though her and Kevin had a normal brother and sister relationship of not really enjoying each other's company at that age.

JOURNEY INTO LOVE

Kevin's sister had a best friend whose name was Lori and who had lived in the same town as us for several years but had since moved away to another town that was about thirty miles away. One weekend that I was spending the night at Kevin's, his sister had Lori over for the weekend as well. To the annoyance of Kevin and his sister, Lori and I started to spend more time talking to each other and sharing our stories. We found our life stories were not so different. We both had dads who enjoyed drinking, worked at automotive plants, and had divorced from our mothers. Both of us were the elder children with younger siblings of the opposite sex. Lori was, and still is, a very pretty woman. I pretty quickly fell head over heels in love. As Lori was nearly two years younger than me, fifteen years old when we met, it was really the first real love for both of us.

To this day, I can recall how my life pretty much changed at that point. The issues at my home somewhat faded into the background as my focus changed to my new girlfriend. It was that all-consuming "soul and heart on fire" first love. Every waking minute, I was either spending time with Lori, talking to her on the phone, or wishing I could be with her. The relationship was a bit difficult because she lived thirty miles away, and with my schedule of work and school, and her schedule of school, band practice, babysitting her younger siblings, it didn't leave a lot of time to see each other every day. The weekends were often spent together and the weekdays spending thirty minutes here or there on the phone each day talking. I remember thinking I had met someone who loves me for me. I also felt that she was far too beautiful to love me and that I was so lucky to have a girlfriend as special as she was.

Lori was two grades younger than me; I was sixteen, and she was fifteen when we met, and she came from a bit more structured household. Her father was present in her life, although in an "every other weekend and one night a week" divorced dad role, and very protective of her. I would think it was fair to say that her father kept a wary eye on me and likely could recall his thoughts and intentions at that age.

Lori and I were pretty inseparable through our high school years, and it was kind of a foregone conclusion that we would eventually be married after we both graduated. Because alcohol and divorce had affected both of us at a young age, we felt strongly that we would not introduce alcohol into our life and would never get divorced if we had kids as we did not want to put them through what we had dealt with growing up.

I think to attempt to protect Lori, after her mom found out that Lori and I had physically consummated our relationship when Lori was still in high school, it was often difficult to see Lori without her parents around. Both our parents had also had children at a young age, so they were concerned that would happen to us and wanted something different for us. From our perspective, her parents were overly strict, and we did what we could to see each other at all costs. This included fake overnights at friends' houses where we instead saw each other and all the stuff that high school kids do when they are consumed in the fire of their first love.

After I graduated high school, I took some classes at a local junior college to try to do the college thing, but after getting a small student loan and not really seeing the benefit of school, I dropped out of college and got a full-time job in the engineering field.

At that time, I was working at a local grocery store and had been promoted to the bakery department making bread, cakes, donuts, and all the sweet things a baker is responsible for. I had moved up the pay scale and was up to about $8 per hour. Not a bad wage in 1984 for a kid just out of high school. After several months in the bakery, getting up at 3:00 a.m. to make the donuts, I realized that this was likely not the life I wanted to pursue as a lifelong career.

Looking through the want ads in the local newspaper, there was no LinkedIn or online job searches at that point, I found a local company who was looking for a blueprint operator and draftsman. Starting pay was a whopping $3.50 per hour, and if they did not have enough engineering work, I would be required to work out in the shop running a drill press, operating a steel saw, or sweeping up the floor. Could I leave the sweetness of the bakery and $8 per hour for this? It was a relatively easy decision for me. I felt that drafting was something I enjoyed, and I knew that one could make a career out of it, and I didn't have to get up until 6:00 a.m., another selling point for me. I told my boss at the bakery I was leaving, and my coworkers were convinced I was crazy for leaving my job and taking one that paid less than half as much. Didn't I know that I could make enough to buy a small home and a car if I stayed in the bakery business? Why would I leave for a job that wasn't guaranteed and that paid half as much?

I think in retrospect, this was one of the key moments in my life where God put me in a direction that I followed based upon faith. I prayed a long time about this decision; though at that time, I would just say that I thought about it for a while. It seemed really clear for me at that time that this was the right choice to make. Throughout my life, in times of difficult and important decisions, God has been there, whether I was conscious of it or not, to help make the path clear. Many times, I have followed the right path, but an equal number of times, when the voice of my own selfishness overpowered that quiet voice in the back of my head, I have taken to path that led to hardship and pain.

After Lori graduated from high school, she also went away to college but dropped out after only a few semesters. She was homesick, we missed each other very much, and she didn't really have a passion for the courses she was taking at the time. We had leaned on each other so much to get through our high school years, and our lives were so intertwined in each other; going off to school and traveling a path that didn't include each other was not something that really interested either of us.

Shacking Up

Today, it is the odd relationship where a couple does not live together before getting married. In the mid-1980s, it was still very much frowned upon by our parents as the normal process was get married, move in together, have children.

After Lori left college, there was really nothing further holding us back from being together each day and each night. We bought a mobile home together from one of her relatives and moved in together. By this point, two years after I had graduated from high school, my engineering career had taken off enough that I was able to afford car payments as well as payments on a mobile home. So by the time I was twenty and Lori was nineteen, we had a home together, were both working, and had started building our life together.

Lori's parents had tried whatever they could to dissuade her from moving in with me. They had told her they would pay for our wedding if we just waited to move in together until after we married. At that point however, we were so much in love and so emmeshed in each other's lives, there was really nothing that was going to stop us from being together.

Getting garage sale furniture, we equipped our new home the best we could, and I was as happy as I had ever been. Though I had moved out of my house as soon as I graduated and moved into a small apartment on my own, living with my love, spending days and nights together, provided a happiness, a satisfaction that was far more than I ever had thought I would attain. I was free from the anger and fights of my childhood home and was living an adult life with a beautiful woman whom I loved deeply.

Lori's parents refusing to pay for our wedding really galvanized her and my attitude of us against the world. No matter what anyone threw at us, what they withheld from us, it didn't matter because we were together, and we would overcome anything. We had helped each other survive adolescence, and we were best friends and lovers and as solid a team as two young kids could be, or so we thought at that time.

When I meet my children's friends who are nineteen and twenty years old, I still look at them as being so very young. I try to recall how mature I thought I was at that age and how much I thought I knew about life, about relationships, about everything, and I just shake my head in amazement. I wonder if these kids feel as smart and confident as I thought I was at that age.

Though we were on our own and both Lori and I were working, me at a conveyor manufacturer for the automotive industry in Detroit, Michigan, and Lori at her mom's answering service, money was plenty tight. Growing up pretty financially constrained (i.e., poor), I didn't need a lot of things, but usually the first thing that would get cut when we were paying the bills was groceries. After paying car payments, rent, utilities, etc., there was often not much left for food. Though this was helpful in allowing me to stay pretty thin, there were a lot of nights of pretty miserable dinners.

Lori and I would take turns making dinner. She had learned some cooking from her mom, and with me growing up in a family of women, I was no slouch in the kitchen and could whip up some pretty creative dishes. Of course, the meals were constrained by what food was available in the refrigerator and pantry at that time. One night, for dinner, I whipped up a special plate of pickles and vanilla frosting. After quartering the pickles and opening the can of frosting, I showed Lori how delicious it was to dip the pickles into the frosting. I quickly learned this was an acquired taste, and Lori really never acquired it. As they say, adversity is the mother of invention, but my mother apparently steered me in a bad direction with that recipe.

Getting Hitched

In the spring of 1988, we decided that we would fulfill what we had dreamt about for a long time and take each other's hand in marriage. As I said, this was what we had been dreaming about since our early high school years and something that we both felt was inevitable and something we both looked forward to.

It was a steaming hot day in May of 1988 when we made our relationship legal in the eyes of the law and our family. We were married in a Lutheran church as a showing of respect for Lori's grandmother who was a strict southern Baptist. Lori was extremely close to her grandmother Clara, and I too loved her grandmother very much. She was a very sweet lady who was always very kind to Lori and me during our entire relationship. That said, she was in no way going to allow or support her granddaughter getting married in a Catholic church. Though she liked me very much, Clara was no fan of Catholics and the Virgin Mary-loving, Pope-supporting faith of Catholicism.

To appease her, and because my faith was only lukewarm at best at that point, we settled on a Lutheran wedding. To me, a twenty-one-year-old kid, it seemed kind of Catholic, and if Lori wasn't going to get married in a Catholic church, I was not going to get married in a Baptist church.

The wedding was everything we could have hoped for. The wedding pictures show what looks to me now as two young kids, barely out of high school, getting married and both deliriously happy.

Having to pay for the wedding ourselves, we didn't have much money for any sort of extravagant honeymoon, so we just took a week off from our jobs and drove down south to start our life and our adventures together. We visited Lori's relatives in Hilton Head, South Carolina. This was a trip where we really fell in love with the climate and the culture of the south and would lead us in years to come to relocate there ourselves.

As I have really and deeply immersed myself in my faith as I've gotten older, I have studied what the sacrament of marriage is intended to be when God is kept at the center of the marriage. I can say at that point in my life when I was first married, I had no real concept of a sacramental marriage. To me at that time, it was a legal contract that bound two people who were deeply in love. I felt that our love for each other was paramount, and that while having a relationship with God was not a bad thing, it was not something I was really focused on at that point, and I couldn't imagine how it was critical to love God more than yourself or your wife. God was someone we were both aware of, and respected, but was not an integral part of our marriage when we were married or throughout the length of our relationship. I loved God as a good Catholic is supposed to but not with the burning, passionate heart on fire type of love I had for my wife and would have for our children. I kind of felt, "Thank you, God, for the blessings, but I don't really need to pray to you or keep you in my marriage to be happy."

We were both excited to begin our life together as a married couple and to eventually have children. We were on the same page with that and knew we wanted to be parents. We would have children and give them a stable life with both parents there to love and raise them. This was something that neither of us had experienced growing up. Neither of us drank alcohol, so we were not going to bring it into our home as we had seen the damage that it had done in our parents' relationship and had learned and were going to do better.

As our marriage grew and we developed as individuals and a married couple, we saw that we both had a pretty solid work ethic. We would work a lot of hours to earn money to acquire stuff that we felt was important. I, probably more than Lori, felt that one thing that was critical was that I provide for my children much more than I had when I was growing up. They were going to have nice clothes, a nice house, and they were not going to get made fun of at school for not having the latest clothes. They would be able to play any sport they wanted, and we would provide them any equipment they need for sports. This often meant I worked a lot of hours because to me at that time, it was very important that my children and my family not go without. I measured my happiness with the stuff I had and what I was able to provide my family. This over importance on material items and outward appearances would lead to a hard fall later in life, but at that time, we were building our lives together and giving our children everything we thought was important.

CHAPTER 6
Children

Having children is one of the most passionate and involving bits of business in human life.
—Siri Hustvedt

New Life

I can say without hesitation that being a father is my greatest accomplishment in life. I understand that it's not that hard and pretty much anyone can do it, but to be able to be part of bringing new life into creation is an awesome and humbling experience.

I think the fact that by the age of twelve I had two fathers that had generally written me out of their life made me determined to try to be the very best father I could be to my children. Though this may not have been a conscious thought for me at that time in my life, I knew that I felt that I had a lot to prove, and that being a good father would help define who I was as a person.

It was just two years, almost to the day, from the time I was married until we had our first child. Born in a hospital in North Charleston, South Carolina, my oldest son entered the world happy and healthy on June 14, 1990.

I had taken a job in South Carolina after Lori and I had fallen in love with the state during our travels. We moved there both because we loved the climate and because we wanted to put some distance between ourselves and our parents and further espouse the "us against the world" theme we had been living for the past few years.

JOURNEY INTO LOVE

Our first move to South Carolina was in 1989, the year after our marriage. Moving across the country for a young married couple seemed like the adventure of a lifetime for me. We would be totally on our own, taking care of ourselves and building new friendships and relationships.

Not having a lot of money, we moved into an apartment complex near the scenic beaches and not far from the touristy Isle of Palms. Everything seemed really great in our lives at that time. We had time to drive around and explore, make new adventures, and had each other to ourselves with no one to share our time with. We were growing and exploring on our own.

It was in the fall of that year, on September 22, 1989, that we experienced one of the most significant adventures of our young married life. That night, due to the convergence of weather patterns over the Atlantic Ocean, Hurricane Hugo roared ashore directly over where our apartment was. The storm tore a path of destruction through the Carolinas that seemed unbelievable to a lifelong northerner like me. I was used to an occasional tornado or a snowstorm that would dump several feet of snow around the city. But the aftereffects of these northern storms were isolated or could be cleaned up with some shovels and plows. I had never seen such devastation as I witnessed from the hurricane.

Knowing that the storm was heading our way and could hit the Carolinas, we hopped in our car and drove inland for several hours to try to avoid the worst of it. Little did we know that the location we chose would be in the direct path of the eye of the storm. Being several hours inland, the storm had weakened a bit when it pounded on our hotel room door, asking to be let in.

The hotel building was shaking and swaying as the waves of wind pounded against the exterior. The glass windows in the living room that normally opened to show a beautiful view of the surrounding palm trees trembled and heaved as the air pressure rose and fell and the rain pelted them incessantly. Sure that the windows were going to explode, we took the mattress off the bed and wedged it against the window to catch any exploding glass. We took the pillows and blankets and lined the bathtub with them. With our makeshift bed in place, Lori tried to lay down in the tub and sleep while I laid on the bathroom floor next to the tub. Certainly, at that point, as in most times of extreme stress, I prayed mightily to a God I hardly spoke to for safe passage through the night for my wife and me.

After what seemed like hours and hours of Mother Nature's anger, the storm subsided, and we were able to move the mattress back to the bed and get a few hours of sleep. As the sun rose, we opened the window to find fallen trees throughout the entire parking lot. Forty-five of the fifty of the cars had been hit by trees that had been toppled by the storm. Our little car, sitting in the middle of the lot, had been spared any damage.

Checking out of the hotel, our next step was to try to get back to our apartment in Goose Creek and see if there was anything left or if we had escaped unscathed yet again. The trip home was one I will never forget. I couldn't imagine, as I looked at the destruction before me, that there were any trees left standing in South Carolina. The route we took to get home was directly through the path the storm had taken just the night before. Today one would say it looked like the background for a zombie apocalypse movie. There were trees down everywhere, power lines across the road, flooding everywhere, and people wandering around with no power and a dazed look on their faces.

Coming back into the city of Charleston, we had to cross a bridge to get back to our side of the bay. Traffic was lined up for what seemed like miles as there was only one lane open on the bridge. As we started across, we saw the police close the bridge directly behind us and not let anyone else across. Apparently there was too much traffic on the adjacent side of the bridge, and the police closed the bridge for what would turn out to be several days. Again, by grace of God, we had just made it, or we would not have been able to get back to our home for several days, and we had no backup plan on where to sleep.

Pulling into the parking lot of the complex, we could see that floodwaters had visited our home while we were gone. Stuff that had seemed securely in place before we left had been uprooted and floated or blown to incredible new locations. There were boats on top of houses, cars under dumpsters, it was completely surreal.

At that point, we were thinking that having a second-floor apartment, so that we would be above the floodwaters, was a pretty lucky move on our part. We slowly opened the apartment door and didn't see a lot of significant damage. The skylight had been torn loose, and we dumped a gallon or so of water out of our VCR unit. That wasn't good but not life-altering. We looked through the house and thought how lucky we had been. As we went to open the master bedroom door, the door would not open. Strange, it was not locked, the handle turned, but it was stuck shut. Finally, after pushing and forcing it with a good bit of strength, I was able to pry the door open a few feet. It was obvious to me then why the door wouldn't open; the roof had caved in and was behind the door. If you have ever opened the door to a room and seen blue sky where roof and ceiling used to be, you can understand how disorienting this can be.

We had made it back to our home, gotten through the storm safely, and called our family and let them know we were okay. Now, we were stuck in a damaged apartment, no power, and no way to get out of town until the roads opened. Being young, we slept on the floor in the living room by the fireplace and found things to keep us busy. Nine months later, our son Alec was born, a Hugo baby.

A Son

I can close my eyes and see clearly the picture that was taken of me holding my son moments after he was born. I can recall the moment as if it was yesterday and not nearly thirty years ago. It was a complete surrender to the amazing miracle that new birth is. I remember crying with my wife when we realized that we had created this beautiful little child that we held in our arms. It didn't seem possible that that something so perfect could come from something that we did. Through God's grace, all his fingers and toes intact and perfect, his fingers miniature replicas of my own, his eyes like his mothers. I was so very grateful to God to have a beautiful and healthy child.

Our parents gave us some time and then came and visited us to help this transition in our lives. Here we were, two kids ourselves, raising a newborn child one thousand miles away from any family. There was no Google, YouTube, or other easy way to look up answers to the million questions that we had. Why was he crying, was he hungry, was he teething, was he sick, what do we do? By being so totally dependent upon us, we were forced to open our two-man team up for one more team member. We were overwhelmed with love for our new child. It was a love unlike any other love I had ever felt in my life. To know that I played a part in creating the tiny life that was in my arms and who relied on me for everything, I was humbled and grateful as never before.

As Alec grew and we become more comfortable as parents, it became a wonderful time in my life. Coming from such a dysfunctional family unit to having a beautiful wife and child and living in a wonderful area of the county, life was indeed good.

We began to miss our family as time went by, and as Alec hit milestones in his development, we realized that as much as we enjoyed being on our own and living it such a wonderful area, we missed being around family to share these experiences with. Our grandparents were getting older, and we wanted our son to know his grandparents and great-grandparents as well.

As Alec had his first birthday, we decided to return to Michigan to be around family and friends. It was a bittersweet time as we were leaving a good job and wonderful and caring new friends, but we looked forward to rekindling old friendships and having help raising our child. The thought of being able to go out for a "date night" while having Grandma and Grandpa watch our child seemed pretty exciting as well.

In South Carolina, to make ends meet financially, both Lori and I worked a couple of jobs. I would work as a plant engineer at an aluminum smelting plant through the week on day shifts. When I would get home, Lori would work evenings at a local Piggly Wiggly supermarket as a cashier. Then, we would both get up at 3:00 a.m. and deliver newspapers. All the time, Alec would be with one or both of us. It was challenging but amazingly rewarding as well knowing that we could do this. We could support ourselves, raise children, have a nice life together. That said, the idea of returning home and having some help occasionally with our child didn't seem like the worst of ideas.

A Second Son

In the fall of 1991, we packed up our belongings and loaded them into a rented moving truck and drove back north to Michigan. If you have ever experienced autumn in Michigan, you know it is a singularly spectacular time of year. The air changes in both temperature and smell. It actually smells like fall and like football. The leaves turn the most beautiful shades of reds and yellows, unlike any other area of the world I have been to. Campfires are lit, apple orchards are visited, and leaves are piled up so kids can jump in them. Fall in Michigan is a special time that everyone should be able to experience. Walking through the woods on a cool autumn night, hand in hand with your love is the stuff that stories are written about.

Unfortunately, fall leads to the barren wasteland of a frozen Michigan winter. That said, there is great comfort and romanticism cuddling up with your significant other in front of a crackling fire in the fireplace on a cold winter night. Returning home and having parents to watch our children, my wife and I were able to rekindle our relationship. Nine months later, on September 12, 1992, our second son, Austin, was born in Howell, Michigan.

After raising our first child through his first two years pretty much on our own, having a second child with family around sure seemed to be easier. All the questions we had the first time were resolved by the time the second child was born. I was a seasoned pro at changing diapers. I had learned that one of the most valuable gifts that a young couple can receive when they have a child is a rocking chair. Many nights I spent in a rocking chair with one of my sons in my arms resting his head on my shoulder as I slowly rocked him to sleep.

As our lives grew busier with raising two young men, we seemed to make less and less time for God in our family. We didn't really go to church except on special occasions, and while we talked in generalities about God and Jesus, I did not have a personal relationship with Him. I heard a homily once in church that God should be at the center of your family and your relationships—you should love God first and your family after that. I thought at that time that certainly the priest who wrote that could not possibly understand what it was like to have your own child and wondered how I could possibly ever love anyone or anything more than my own children. Only after thirty years of falling into and out of love in different relationships and seeing that God has always been and will always be there to love me unconditionally, I see that all my other relationships are better formed and more loving when I keep God at the center of my heart and the center of my relationships with others. God's love magnifies itself and reflects off my heart toward others when I am open to Him.

Growing Up

As the boys grew, our bond of love and friendship grew more and more each year. I felt like their dad but also their buddy as well. I guess my lack of brothers and male relationships when I was growing up manifested itself in my relationship with my sons. Often, to my wife's chagrin and at times anger, she felt like she had three boys to discipline, and often she was made the butt of our "male humor." She was a very good mother to the boys, and they are blessed to have had her as a parent to balance out my silliness with her caring and calming demeanor.

From a young age, the boys and I were always pretty competitive with each other. We played pretty much any and all sports and wrestled and roughhoused enough that it made the grandparents anxious when we were around. I must have heard a hundred times "not to play so rough with the boys," but they loved it, and we usually had a great time. Usually only a few items of houseware were broken at any one event. There were the practical jokes at each other's expense, and often their mom's expense.

Two examples occurred, and we realized the boys had become a bit too competitive and had to learn the extent of when jokes went beyond being funny. We were taking a family bike ride around the neighborhood one summer afternoon. Growing up in a small town in Michigan, we could often get on the bikes and just peddle around town and around the subdivision for a little exercise and family time together. On this specific afternoon, we were riding along a lightly trafficked paved street near home. My youngest son thought it might be funny to bump his bicycle wheel against his mother's to shake her up a bit. As he slowly lined up the tires and slid his front tire into her rear tire, it all went horribly wrong. Somehow her tire got locked up, and she went head over heels over the front of the bike and landed on the pavement as my son biked away. I think he realized at that point, that joke might not have turned out how he had planned. After Lori uttered more than a few curse words and threats about what she would do if she ever caught him, she pulled her bruised and bloodied legs off the pavement and remounted the bike for the longest ride home we ever had. It was a terrible thing to see but kind of like those funniest home video shows. God help me if I couldn't laugh at it. Seeing her wipe out and then seeing me trying to hide back a laugh certainly made for a very long day for the whole family.

As if learning to compete with the boys was something it took a while to understand, Lori decided to have a Rollerblading race with my oldest son. My son Alec took to both ice-skating and Rollerblading at a pretty young age and fancied himself an accomplished skater while still in elementary. So, when he challenged his mom to a race, I didn't figure it would turn out too well. The premise was pretty straightforward, race down the street to the first side street then turn around and race back to the driveway. It seemed like a good challenge between mother and son. The race started out pretty well, and to my surprise, Mom was amazingly quick on the blades and reached the side street just ahead of Alec. They made the turn and headed home to the finish line at the end of the driveway. With about one hundred feet to go, I think Alec realized he was going to lose. He was going to lose to his mom, and he would never hear the end of that, so out of the blue, he stuck out his hockey stick into her blades and sent her flying across the concrete. He skated victoriously past her and finished in first place as yet another string of curse word flew forth from the mouth of his beloved mother.

I think at this point, the boys' mother and I realized two things, I may have raised them a bit too competitive, and two, never race with the boys unless you wear headgear and elbow pads.

Though we didn't have a lot of money when the boys were growing up, I think we were solidly middle class and had a nice house in a decent small-town community. One of the luxuries we had pretty much all the boy's formative years was a family membership to a local gym. This gym was, to this day, the nicest gym I have ever been a member of. It had everything one would want in a gym. It had free weights for lifting, a quarter-mile indoor track, pool, jacuzzi, sauna, racquetball and basketball courts, and more. It was a haven of activity for growing boys and dads who refused to grow up. Lori and I often discussed whether we could afford this gym membership, but we always tried to maintain our membership there as it was a great way to spend time together as a family. Whether lifting with my sons or playing racquetball, hanging out in the sauna, it was a great healthy way to spend time together and grow our relationship while advocating a healthy lifestyle. Sometimes the competitiveness would rear up, and a simple game of racquetball would turn in "prison ball" where there were no rules, and it was okay to knock over the other guy as he was getting ready to hit the ball. Often the gym workers would walk by and wonder what the heck we were doing. When we brought the boxing gloves to the gym and started sparring with each other in a racquetball court or aerobics studio, signs were instantly printed and posted that members were not allowed to bring boxing gloves to the gym. I called it the Rymarz rule.

CHAPTER 7
On the Move

I find the great thing in this world is not so much where we stand, as in what direction we are moving: To reach the port of heaven, we must sail sometimes with the wind and sometimes against it—but we must sail, and not drift, nor lie at anchor.
—Oliver Wendell Holmes, Sr.

Relocating for Work

It was a lovely Tuesday morning as I looked out the window of the construction trailer where my office was located. The ocean blue skies were cloudless, and the day had started like so many others before. Get up early and drive into work across the Red River bridge that connected Bossier City to Shreveport where I had relocated my family to for my job at General Motors.

The boys had gotten up at the usual time and had taken the bus to school. Alec in middle school and Austin in elementary, they had adjusted well to the move; they were resilient as most young kids are and had made new friends pretty quickly.

It was around 8:00 a.m., September 11, 2001, and I was already in my first meeting of the day planning for the days construction activities when a colleague came into the meeting room and let us know that someone had mistakenly flown a plane into a building in New York or somewhere and that it was showing up on all the news channels in their construction trailer. Without thinking too much about it, we continued the meeting and figured someone had been flying a small private plane and had a medical emergency and hoped that not too many people had gotten hurt.

It wasn't more than ten minutes later when people's cell phones started ringing in the meeting, and everyone started talking among themselves that yet another plane had hit a building. What in the world as going on? What a coincidence that this would happen twice in the same day. Our colleague burst in through the door and shouted to us that we all had to come over to his office trailer and watch the news; we wouldn't believe what was happening.

Slowly, we got up and walked over to the adjacent trailer wondering what all this commotion was about. It was then we saw the iconic videos of the large commercial airliners flying into the World Trade Centers. When the news came across that a plane had flown into the Pentagon, a shudder finally went up my spine that we were under attack, and I started to wonder how close to home this would hit. Was my family okay?

I immediately called my wife. Lori was at home after getting the kids off to school and cleaning up and had just heard the news herself. The pest control service had come to the door, and the guy had asked her if she would turn on the TV so they could watch what was going on. As a parent, Lori's immediate thoughts after watching the news were that we needed to get the kids and get them home until we understood what was going on and how far reaching it was.

It was then when this tragedy really hit home. The local news channels came on with their coverage of this event, and we were informed that the schools where our children were attending were on lockdown and no parents would be allowed to get the children at this time.

Unbeknownst to us, our decision to purchase a home in the Bossier City, a short drive to Shreveport yet a wonderful family-oriented community, put us within close proximity to Barksdale air force base. It was that fateful morning that President Bush was flown to Barksdale, under jet fighter escort, and local businesses went on lockdown. As I spoke to Lori, we could hear the jet fighters roaring ferociously low and loud over our home. "What was that?" I asked nervously.

"Those are jet fighters and Air Force One flying over our backyard," said Lori with a tinge of fear in her voice. She had been on the way to the local store to pick up cupcakes for Austin's birthday the next day when the low-flying Air Force One, so close she could almost look into the windows of the plane, caused her to immediately turn around and head home.

The thought the United States was under attack and the leader of our country was less than ten minutes away from where our children were on lockdown in school was a terrifying thought for us as parents. What if whoever did this knew the president was here in Bossier City and decided to attack Barksdale like they had done the Pentagon? There was so much confusion and fear that morning that we had no idea what was going to happen next. It was with great relief that I finally got the call from my wife that she had been allowed to go to the school and pick up the children and was headed home. She was going to get everyone inside, lock up the doors, and wait for me to get home. They had attacked us by air; were there more localized attacks to follow? The fear and hysteria of that day will never be forgotten, even for someone who was so far disconnected from New York, Washington, or Shanksville, Pennsylvania, where these tragedies occurred.

Welcome to our new home and the joys of relocating the family for work. This fateful day affected so many, maybe everyone, around the country to some extent or another. Many lost their lives that day, and many continue to struggle with the aftermath. Had we stayed in Michigan, we would not have had the experiences we did that day, but the choices we make resonate in our lives and the lives of others for years to come.

Having been assigned to work on a new construction project for General Motors, I was advised that the project would go for several years as GM had allocated close to a billion dollars to upgrade this facility in Shreveport, Louisiana, to build a new small truck. I had the choice of flying back and forth for the next few years or relocating my family to the area. Flying around the country for work may at first seem glamorous to some. The thoughts that come to most people when thinking of traveling are of staying in nice hotels, getting nice rental cars, racking up frequent flyer points. But in fact, for those that travel extensively for work, and there are ever more living this lifestyle, it is a grind—late or missed flights, lost luggage, time away from family. Having lived this road warrior lifestyle previously, I knew it was a fairly easy decision for my wife and I that we would prefer to relocate the family so we could be together for the next few years. The kids were young enough that they were both excited and a little nervous for the move. We promised them that when we moved, we would get a house with a swimming pool and jacuzzi so that it would seem like a fun adventure for them.

Rajun Cajuns

We really didn't know what we were getting ourselves into when we moved to Louisiana. I had lived all over the south by that point in my life. I had lived in South Carolina, Texas, and Alabama by then and had come to appreciate southern culture. There is a noticeable difference in the attitude of people once you head south past the Mason Dixon line. Going in with an open mind, I grew to very much appreciate the pace in the south along with the openness and hospitality I had always experienced. Knowing all that, I learned Louisiana had a culture and feel all its own.

After looking at several choices, we bought a beautiful home in Bossier City, Louisiana. We had looked at many homes but really fell in love with this one when we saw it. It was a large ranch with ceramic tile floors throughout. It was spacious and had the kids' bedrooms on one side of the house and the master bedroom on the other side. To stay true to our promise to our children, the house had both an inground pool and an enclosed gazebo with a jacuzzi. The kids loved it as soon as they saw it. Moving with GM, or likely most large companies, was relatively painless as they hired a professional moving company to pack up and move everything for us. Having done several cross-country moves our self in our younger married days, packing everything into the backs of pickups and hoping nothing would blow out when driving down the highway, and now having professionals come in and move everything into a real moving truck seemed like a real luxury.

I don't think we had been in the house for more than a day or two before my sons had met other boys their age and had already started playing street hockey, Rollerblading, and bicycling with them. All the caution we take as adults when we meet new people, guarded by years of armor we have built up to protect ourselves from getting hurt, none of that is there when you are young. You fling headlong into friendships not expecting or requiring any certain behaviors. As a parent, it was great to see the boys make new friends so quickly.

One of the benefits we hoped to attain from this move was an increase in diversity into the boys' lives. Growing up where they had, the boys were close to family but were also in school with a lot of kids that looked a lot like themselves. We wanted the boys to grow up in a more diverse environment so that they would see that all people are created equally, and no person is superior to another based upon skin color, religious beliefs, or other visual differences.

We were extremely happy to see that shortly after starting school, one of the boys asked if he could have a friend over to swim and hang out. When the young man that came over was African American, we were happy that the kids never thought twice about asking if a "black kid" could come over. They just asked if a friend could come over. While it is naïve to say we don't see color or differences, it is fair to say that they did not recognize this difference as a big enough issue that they even needed to mention it. It was just another friend they had made at school. I am so proud of my kids that to this day, I don't think they have ever had issues with anyone strictly because of their race or religion. I think the lessons I learned from my parents and grandparents that we should not judge people by their appearance was, gratefully, passed on to my children.

As the kids made more friends at school, we as parents were introduced to new things as well. The kids helped us to grow and expand. They asked if we would we be interested in going to one of their friend's house to attend a crawfish boil? What the heck was that? Did we want to attend a Mardi Gras parade with their friends and watch the floats in the parade? The Cajun culture really grew on us, and we came to love the unique flavor and bigger-than-life colors and pageantry of Louisiana.

We also found a very nice church to attend while living in Bossier City. The Cathedral of St. John Berchmans on Jordan Street felt like home the minute we walked through the heavy wooden doors. Entering, you see directly in front of you the raised white marble altar and the beautiful gothic-style vaulted ceilings and stained glass. Greeted the first time we entered by welcoming parishioners made all the difference in the world. We developed a very nice Sunday morning routine. We would drop the kids off at Sunday school, and my wife and I would go to a local coffee shop for a morning pick-me-up of caffeine and a sweet. We would talk about the week past, the week ahead, and generally reconnect after a week of work. Then, picking the kids up from Sunday school, we would attend mass and then head to the local buffet for Sunday lunch. Getting home would take us less than ten minutes, and we would all be changed into our swimming gear and hit the pool for an afternoon of playing and relaxing. It was a great way to spend our Sundays and reconnect as a family.

A Wondering Soul

As I reflect, the desire and joy of moving around, and traveling in general, may have been imbued into my soul at a young age. According to the United States Census Bureau, the average American moves eleven times in their life. I had achieved that number by the time I was in my early twenties. Some of the moves were necessitated by my parents' desire to move into better neighborhoods, and others were my own desire to see the country. Regardless, I never really felt a strong desire to plant roots solidly in any certain area. This wandering spirit did make it difficult when someone would ask me where I'm from or where I grew up. I typically talk in generalities, such as, I mostly grew up in Michigan. This wanderlust hit full bloom when I reached my early fifties, and I decided to fully embrace the adventure of travel and sold my house, gave away most of my belongings, and bought an RV. Now, with no physical address anywhere, I am free to travel the country and get up and move locations as the spirit moves me. This is a story for another chapter however.

 I was blessed, or maybe destined, to work in a job that fully supported and rewarded my desire to travel. Starting in my late twenties, I transitioned from the role of a mechanical engineer who would sit, originally behind a drafting board and then a computer workstation, to design new pieces of machinery and equipment to help automate the factory floor. It was while I was in my late twenties and working for a German automotive supplier when my boss called me and another individual into his office. He needed a project manager for a new paint shop project that Mercedes Benz was building in Alabama and asked if either of us be interested in this role. It would require travel both stateside and internationally and would be more of a management role than engineering. It was a pretty easy call for me, and my colleague had no desire to take on this type of assignment, so as simply as that, I had moved into a new job assignment. Throughout my life, both professionally and personally, God has been present to make these sort or opportunities present and has often helped direct me in my choices. Though at that time I was making these sort of life choices I would not have had the spiritual presence to reflect and pray about it, I likely said I would do it in less than two minutes; God has been a kind and caring Father to me and helped direct me in ways and for reasons I cannot understand, other than that He loves me, and all His children, with a deep and abiding love.

 Throughout my career, I took on new assignments and moved to new jobs, either by choice or necessity. Several of the small companies I worked for went out of business, and I learned to believe and trust in myself and my abilities and not depend upon the company to take care of me. I saw quickly that the companies I worked for would provide me fair pay and benefits when the economy and times were good but would do what was required when they were required to make tough choices. In retrospect, losing my job twice, early in my career, due to the company I was working for shutting their doors and going bankrupt, made me realize I needed to work hard and make myself marketable through my skillset. Often in my youth I attributed my modest financial success to my hard work and wise career choices. As I matured in my faith, I came to thank God for my ability to work hard and for being rewarded for this hard work. I was always, thanks to God, able to physically work very hard. As I travelled around the world however, I saw many, many people that put my work ethic to shame, and they were never rewarded financially to be able to support their families simply because of the situation and economic structure they had been born into. All I have accomplished is truly a blessing from God.

My love of traveling often put me into positions where I really needed to learn and grow to be successful. I have always enjoyed a good challenge, and traveling abroad, thirty years ago, before the advent of modern technology was certainly a challenge. When I accepted the project manager assignment for the German paint shop supplier, one of my first tasks was to visit the home office in Stuttgart, Germany, to meet the team and get leveled up for the upcoming project. "Why don't you fly there next week and meet with the team and see how far along they are?" my boss casually suggested to me about five minutes after I accepted the role. Fly over there? Meet the team? Where in the world was Stuttgart, and how would I get there? What had I gotten myself into?

After assuring my boss that this seemed like a great idea and I would make it happen, I slowly walked out of his office and directly to his assistant and asked her everything she knew about international travel and how I could manage to get to Germany next week for a visit. After spending several minutes with me, I had the rudimentary information I needed to make my trip plans. There would be no one to meet me at the airport, and I would be on my own to make my way across Germany to meet my new team members. I would fly into Frankfurt, rent a car, and drive to Stuttgart to the home office. Never mind I had no maps of Germany, didn't speak a bit of German, and didn't even have the address of the home office, I would make it happen. I knew in general I would have to drive south from Frankfurt to get to the office and figured if I came across the Swiss or Austrian border, I would have gone too far and would turn around and head back into Deutschland.

Luckily, when I arrived, the folks at the airport spoke enough English that I was able to rent a car and get the trip started. Since this trip occurred before the advent of cell phones made it somewhat important for me to have a good plan and a few German Marks in case I needed to call for directions, or a rescue team. Traveling across the country, I quickly came to appreciate German engineering (I had gotten a Mercedes convertible to drive), their highway system (unlimited speed limit on the Autobahn), and what the German words were for "exit ramp," "entrance ramp," and "rest area." The country was beautiful, and as I traveled south through cities I had learned about in school, Darmstadt, Heidelberg, Heilbronn, I fell in love with international travel and learning about and experiencing new cultures. "Be careful in Germany," I was told as the people may be friendly but are very reserved and not open to strangers. As I eventually arrived in the city of Stuttgart, I became hopelessly lost driving around the motorways in the city. I was apparently so obviously lost that a German fellow approached me. "Careful," I said to myself, stranger danger in full effect. After speaking to me in German and seeing my eyes glaze over slightly, he asked in broken English, "You are lost, my friend?"

Why yes, yes, I am, is it that obvious? I thought to myself.

"Where you look to go?"

"I am looking for this company on Zuffanhausen Street," I responded. Had he heard of it I wondered.

"Yah, yah, I know this place. Follow me, and I will take you there," he kindly offered. Where was the reserved, cold German attitude I had read about? This gentleman was going to go out of his way and take his time to help a total stranger, a foreigner no less, to find their way. It was pretty quickly after this experience that I realized I needed to form my own opinions of people that I met in different cultures and that the stereotypes and descriptions of people and cultures that I had learned in school were written in generalities by people who often may have never visited the countries they were writing about. I learned quickly I would be doing myself a disservice if I generalized entire cultures by the one paragraph I had read about them while I was sleeping through my high school classes where we talked about this.

Go West, Young Man

As I continued to travel around to different countries and throughout the United States, my confidence in my ability to figure out the situation and work through any difficulties became greater and greater. I felt like I was becoming a seasoned traveler and did not hesitate to take any trip for work or with my family as time allowed. It was with the burgeoning navigational confidence that I suggested to my wife that for the summer of 2003, when the kids had gotten out of school for the year, we should pack everyone up in our van and take a road trip to the west coast and visit the national parks along the way.

At first, a bit incredulous at the idea, my wife asked how we would go about doing this with everyone. Would we stay in hotels, who would watch the family dog, how long would we need to take to get to California and back to Michigan, could we get everyone's schedule to be free for summer sports, work, and other activities to make this happen? These were all great questions, so we were glad that we started planning this many months before summer arrived.

During the time I started to plan this trip, there were no Goggle maps, Waze, TripAdvisor, or any of the many travel tools we now take for granted, and truthfully, that was a big part of the fun of it. Downloading maps and printing them off and marking them up became a shared adventure; though, I will admit I was the one who really enjoyed this part of the trip planning. I recall with fondness however how I would give the boys a travel atlas and have them read me directions as to which highway I should get on, how far to the next turnoff, any cool points of interest along the way." I guess God's presence in our lives is much like a travel atlas. He gives us, through our conscience, the right path to take if we only decide to follow the directions. Though we may not know how far the road we are currently on will take us, He promises many beautiful sights along the way if we take a moment to lift our eyes up from the daily grind we put ourselves in and simply stop, roll down the window of life, and smell the fresh air and look at the beauty that surrounds us at every moment. This beauty may often be hidden, like a flower that is growing behind the shrubs that is only seen when we look a bit deeper or the smile of a person who is eating at a soup kitchen but takes time to laugh and joke with others who are there, a nurse who jokes with the hospice patient who knows they have but a few months to live and is scared but appreciates a moment of levity. All these were instances of beauty that have been present in my life when I but stopped to push back the weeds that were blocking my view.

As the time to depart on our epic family road trip approached, I think it is pretty fair to say that everyone was looking forward to the adventure that lay ahead of us. Not really knowing what to expect, as it was for all of us our first trip this far west, we felt the sense of taking off on a family adventure to unknown parts was exciting. At that time, the boys would have been twelve and ten and really old enough to appreciate what they were about to experience, while still young enough to get bored with the van ride as we forged ahead through thousands of miles of the US backroads and highways. Much to my unwarranted dismay, the boys had handheld Gameboys and a TV video game system that we hooked up to the drop-down TV that was installed in the conversion van we owned. I knew there would be hours upon hours of endless roads that we would travel, so I knew having a diversion for the kids would keep them from asking the question all parents dread, "How much longer until where there?" But I became unnecessarily upset when they would continue to play the game as we drove by a national monument or historic landmark that I was sure they would be greatly enriched by if they would just put down the video game for a few minutes.

After a few arguments and, I'm sure, harsh words from me, I did not reasonably measure my words or the pain they could render at that time. I would let them play and just tell them they were going to regret not seeing this historic marker. As it turned out, they grew up to be well adjusted adults, and the lack of seeing that monument I felt was so important did not really affect their lives as deeply as I warned them it would.

As we set out on our journey, I kind of felt inside how much this trip would mean to us all in the future. It is not often that a middle-income working family can pack up the kids and head across the country for three weeks. As it turned out, it would end up being the only time that we did a family road trip of this magnitude. Knowing this would likely be something we all remembered for some time, I started a couple of handwritten journals as soon as we left. I had two journals, one for my wife and I and one for the kids and asked that we all try to write in them throughout the trip to capture our experiences. In retrospect, I am glad that we thought of this idea. The journal entries from all of us are still snippets of that adventure that I can look back on to this day and recall with fondness the joy of that shared family experience.

Looking back at the journal, I see we left Michigan for the start of our trip on June 6, 2003, at 11:45 a.m. I am sure that I had planned to leave by 11:00 a.m., and I was upset and anxious because we were forty-five minutes behind the schedule I had in my head but probably failed to tell anyone else. A planner likes to plan and gets anxious when his plan is not followed by others, even if they likely weren't necessarily told what the plan was. I can't imagine how many hours in my life I have wasted by being upset that we left five minutes after I had wanted. How many times I have rushed around and been angry at those I love because I was afraid we would be late for some event only to show up fifteen minutes beforehand, but I wanted to be there twenty minutes early so we had time to do whatever. These days I would say to my sons and those that wanted to listen, let the small stuff go, and don't stress over it. Enjoy every second you have with those that you love. There will be enough opportunities to be angry with each other for significant issues; don't let the small stuff overwhelm you and take time away from loving each other.

Being an engineer and planner at heart, I also see from looking back at my first journal entry it was sixty-five degrees when we left, and we had 49,872 miles on the odometer of our van as we backed it out of our driveway. No detail was too small to capture. The best part for me now as I read back through these journals are not what I wrote but reading the thoughts of everyone as they experienced this trip. After stopping at so many beautiful national parks along the way—the Badlands, Mt. Rushmore, Yellowstone, Moab, Joshua Tree, the Grand Canyon, just to name a few—I am so grateful to God that I was able to take my children on a trip like this. To this day, after our trips to Hawaii for their senior trips and all the other places we have been blessed to visit, both of the boys still reflect back on this trip, and even though they missed so much by not listening to me and playing those video games, they still say that was the best trip of their lives. As a parent, you can't really ask for more than to be able to give them wonderful memories like that.

Have Suitcase, Will Travel

Upon returning to our "real life" after this trip out West, my job of global coordination at General Motors really took off, and I was assigned to work on the global conveyor team. Looking back at my career through the vantage point of an entire view of my work encounters, I realized it is easy to see that the experience I had traveling globally were the fondest in my professional life. I was blessed to visit so many countries and meet so many wonderful, caring, and talented people. Being open and receptive to what each culture had to offer me allowed me to cut through the preconceived notions that so many had of the various countries I was blessed to visit. Being able to walk through the safari lands of South Africa, travel through the inner city of Bogota, Columbia, drive past the pyramids of Giza on my way to work each morning, spend weekends in Europe climbing the Alps in Switzerland, or taking the train from Dresden, Germany, to Prague were all adventures I was able to experience in my time at General

Motors. While working for a large corporation can sometimes lead you to feel like you are simply a cog in the machine, working for a large multinational global corporation can also provide wonderful experiences like these if you are open to them and not fearful of learning new and challenging things.

One of the most significant and life-changing work assignments I had was when I was asked to provide technical support for a new paint shop expansion at General Motors facility in Egypt. Located just outside the main city of Cairo in 6th of October City, the plant was old and dated and not able to meet the new volume requirements the corporations marketing department felt were required to increase profitability.

A significant expansion to the existing paint shop facilities was approved and funded by GM leadership. We would utilize a certain type of conveyor equipment that we in GM US had jointly developed with our colleagues in GM Europe, GM Brazil, and GM Asia Pacific. Because of the large dollar amount spent in the United States to upgrade facilities, we had utilized the majority of these new systems and were thus most familiar with them. My experience as the lead mechanical engineer in the United States on these systems and my affinity for traveling seemed to make it a logical choice, I assume, for my group's leadership to ask me if I minded working on the GM Egypt project in a technical support role. Little did I know by saying yes, I would be saying yes to God opening up many new doors in my heart and soul.

The project would be led by the GM Brazil group out of their headquarters in Sao Caetano. The supplier that was awarded this project was based in Milan, Italy, and the end user was, of course, in Egypt. At the start of this project, both the suppliers and the GM Egypt engineers came to America to visit some of our plants where we had these new systems in place so they could see them and meet the plant teams to get their feedback. Later on in the project, we would also visit the GM plant in Zaragoza, Spain, to look at these system as they were being installed so the Egypt team could see them both in use and being installed new. Many of our design meetings were held in Milan, Italy, at the supplier's offices. To sit in meetings that included Italians, Egyptians, Brazilians, and Americans was a wonderful experience that I will always remember. These meetings were so very different and exciting compared to the traditional design meetings I had sat through in the United States. Of course, the meetings were held in the common language that everyone pretty much knew, English. This was extremely helpful to me as an American. My colleagues told me many jokes during these meetings; this one I still remember, "What do you call someone who speaks two languages? Bilingual. What do you call someone who speaks three languages? Trilingual. What do you call someone who speaks just one language? American."

I was amazed that everyone around the table spoke a minimum of two languages and often three or four. My ability to clearly communicate as I travelled the world was significantly affected by my limited linguistic skills. I was blessed to be able to hear and quickly pick up new languages, but as with any skill, if you don't use what you have learned frequently, you lose that skill.

To see how engineers from around the world approached the technical and financial problems we were faced with was enlightening as well. While budgets were always a concern when working on a project in the United States, the budgets in the emerging markets where margins were smaller and labor costs were so much less were a fraction of those in the United States. To see some of the unique and cost-effective solutions that were proposed by my engineering counterparts from Brazil and Egypt made me a better engineer. To see the creative flair the Brazilians and Italians used when solving issues made me believe that our creations didn't have to be straight lines and geometry but could be artistic as well. These experiences working with "less experienced" technical teams made me both a better engineer and a better person.

Part of getting to understand the requirements of this new equipment was to spend significant time on the plant floor at the facility in 6th of October City, Egypt, to meet the people who would install the equipment, who would maintain it, and who be using it every day as production operators. Along with understanding the work-related part of this assignment, I was also able to share in discussions about life, politics, and religion. There is a saying about never talking about politics and religion at work, but in Egypt, they were so intertwined into the daily fabric of their lives, it was almost impossible not to discuss these items. The leader of the country at the time was Hosni Mubarak, and this was before the January 25 revolution of 2011.

Politics has never much interested me. Whether in the United States or abroad, I have a generally unfavorable opinion of politics and politicians. I do believe that some, optimistically maybe most, get into politics because they want to make a favorable difference for their community. Far too many however seem to get into politics because of uncontrollable narcissism and the abundant money that seems to be available through political action committees and various fund-raising groups. My experience has been that this dynamic is prevalent throughout the world, and thus, politics holds little sway over my day-to-day thoughts.

Religion, on the other hand, has always held a special place in my heart and soul and fascinates me to no end. The lasting memories I have of Egypt are of the kindness of the people I met and the devotion to their faith. It was this devotion that really rekindled the flame of love in my heart for Jesus Christ. Relighting this flame took a circuitous route through the Koran and Mohammed, but it forever changed my life.

As I arrived in Egypt, I, like most first-time visitors, was overwhelmed with the overload of inputs to my senses. The sounds, the smells, the sights, and the tastes were unlike anything I had ever experienced. I had seen sand dunes but never deserts so vast. I had felt heat but never the skin-melting temperatures that permeated the interior of even the best air-conditioned cars and hotel rooms. I drove by sights that I had only seen in magazines and TV shows. The sphinx, the Pyramids of Giza, the Nile river were all part of my new daily routine.

I also saw man-made mountains of brick and concrete that I learned were called minarets and were illuminated in beautiful green lights each night. At dusk and throughout the day, loud voices of praise would arise across the Nile and through the bustling city streets. The sound was loud enough to be heard no matter where you went. I learned quickly that these calls to prayer, or *salat* in Arabic, would occur five times daily, and when you heard them, you understood that much of everything else stopped and the faithful would roll out their prayer rugs, get on their knees, praying in the direction of Mecca, and would give praise to Allah.

As a cradle Catholic who was raised in my faith but attended church only once a week and maybe said a mealtime prayer occasionally, to see this dedication to their faith shook me to my core. I immediately knew that this level of prayerful dedication to their beliefs is what I had been unknowingly longing for my entire life. I felt a bit betrayed. Why did the Catholic faith not give its 1.3 billion faithful members the opportunity to pray like this? Why did we as Roman Catholics lack this dedication to our Father, Son, and Holy Spirit, the blessed Trinity I learned about in grade school catechism?

I immediately engaged my closest Egyptian friends about their beliefs in Islam and learned about the integration of their beliefs into their daily routines. I asked and was kindly given the opportunity to visit and pray at the mosque of Muhammad Ali, the Alabaster Mosque, in Cairo, Egypt. Like the great Catholic cathedrals I had seen in my travels in Italy, Germany, and throughout Europe, I was overwhelmed and humbled at the beauty of this mosque. I was able to sit and kneel in prayer in the mosque and ask God why I had not been made aware of this depth of prayer prior to this time and to thank Him for removing the scales from my eyes. I had not seen a light and fallen off a horse, like my namesake St. Paul, but the local camels could have been the backdrop for my conversion story.

I talked to my friends further about their beliefs. Perhaps I would become a Muslim so I could join in daily prayers and better integrate my faith into my life. I really needed to study this faith and see what it was about. Islam was turning out to be nothing like the radical faith I had learned about through the American media outlets. I learned about the five pillars of the faith, about the Holy month of Ramadan and the ascetic practices of the faithful out of reverence for their prophet and their God. I was hooked; this is the level of faith that I wanted in my life.

But wait, I found one little the issue. To become a Muslim, I would have to accept that Jesus Christ was not the Son of God but was in fact just another great prophet in the line of Moses, Abraham, and would be succeeded by yet another prophet, Mohammed. I would have to accept that the twelve apostles knew of this and perpetrated the hoax that they had seen him rise from the grave three days after his death, all the way to their own martyrdom over this hoax. Eleven of these twelve would eventually suffer martyrdom over their belief and preaching that Jesus was in fact crucified on the cross and rose from the dead, and none of these eleven apostles recanted their story to save their own life. I could not make the step, cross the literal line in the sand, that I would reject what I had learned about Jesus to allow me to fully embrace the Islamic faith.

This left me in quite the quandary. I wanted a faith as devoted as Islam, but I didn't share the basic tenants of their faith. This monumental threshold that I crossed however did force me to look much closer at my own faith than I had ever looked before. My heart and my soul were on fire for a love of God that I had never experienced before. In time, I would come to understand that in fact, the earliest Christians, continued the practice of their Jewish forefathers of reciting prayers at certain times of the days. These prayer times and prayers themselves, the psalms and eventually readings from the Gospel, would fully develop into the Breviary or the Divine Office or Liturgy of the Hours. Catholics did in fact have a way of stopping everything that was going on in their daily routine and praying to God. What I found that was different was that it was primarily those in monastic communities—I didn't even know that there were still Catholic monks—and also diocesan priests, who recited these prayers. The regular faithful Catholics that I knew and saw in church in Sunday were not required to recite these prayers. Many were and are still not aware that this ancient form of prayer still exists and is alive in our faith. How is it that I could have attended catechism for at least ten years and had families on both my mother's and father's side that were committed Catholics, and yet I had never heard of the Liturgy of the Hours is something that still puzzles me. This revelation of a new depth of prayer changed my life and forced me to make many difficult choices as I grew and matured in my new two-thousand-year-old faith.

CHAPTER 8
The Fall from Grace

It is good for me that Thou has humbled me,
that I may learn Thy commandments.
—The Rule of St. Benedict, Psalm CXVIII

First there is the fall, and then we recover from
the fall. And both are the mercy of God.
—St. Julian of Norwich

Hiding from God's Light

Thomas Merton was a well-known monk who lived in the Trappist Monastery of Gethsemani in rural Kentucky. In the early and mid-1960s, prior to his untimely death while in Asia in 1968, he was the novice master at the abbey of Gethsemani. Part of his responsibility as novice master was to teach the incoming Cistercian novices, those who had not made final vows as monks yet, about the Rule of St. Benedict as well as other monastic teachings and requirements. Thankfully for those of us who are interested, many of these lectures were recorded and are now available for us to listen to as well. For Benedictine oblates like myself who study and seek to live their lives by the Rule of St. Benedict, as it applies to our status in life, these talks from Thomas Merton are invaluable lessons from one of the spiritual masters of our time. As I found out, the lessons Merton taught fifty years ago apply to me as I struggled through my life as well. A particular lesson he taught that reflected the reality of my life was that,

> To ascend, we must first descend. If you find yourself ascending without descending, you are mistaken. In proportion to us experiencing ourselves going down, descending, we go up. If we experience that we are ascending, then we are going down.

In less theological terms and more easily understood is the lesson taught today by all twelve-step programs in that one cannot begin to heal, to ascend, until they have reached their bottom, rock bottom as popularly stated.

Throughout my life, I had ascended the ladder of success at work. I had gotten higher and higher promotions and positions that recognized my hard work. My ego was swollen with praise from others personally and professionally for what I had believed that I had achieved through my own talents and hard work, with no nod to God for giving me the gifts that allowed me to achieve anything whatsoever. Experiencing this ascent, this ego-driven ride to the top, led in a very real and painful way to me and many of my loved ones who were hurt by my descent into drinking, personal selfishness, and marital infidelity. Throughout this descent, God never left my side, but I turned more and more of a deaf ear to Him as I sought to fulfill my own desires. These were not the sins of someone who had led a pious life and then went off the rails; no, the fall from grace, sparked by the concupiscence of man and fueled by my own sins, started at an early age.

Though I was in love at a young age with my wife to be, it seemed like I was always looking for something else and never completely satisfied with the beauty and fullness of the relationship I was in at the present time. When Lori and I first met and up until our children were in elementary school, we did not attend church on a regular basis. I was a Catholic but didn't have a real relationship with God other than knowing He created the universe and that there would be repercussions for my actions, either positive or negative, once I died. God was not a part of my daily or weekly routine as the decisions I made and the lack of consideration for others, the whole

"Love thy neighbor" commandment, were not something I regularly thought of.

When I graduated high school, my girlfriend, Lori, had just finished her sophomore year of high school and had a few years left. At that time, I had considered joining the air force. I had seen a few movies, and I was pretty sure it would be cool to be a pilot. Never mind that I had neither the grades nor any idea of what it took to become a pilot. I saw movies of fighter pilots doing stunts in their planes and thought that might not be a bad life. Lori let me know without hesitation that if I signed up for the air force, she didn't see herself waiting for four years for me to get out of the service. While at that time I couldn't imagine not having her as a girlfriend, my self-esteem was so low I was sure I wouldn't find anyone else; I understand now that what she told me was both truthful and reasonable. Then it seemed like an ultimatum, and I chose not to join the air force. As I said, I realize now that I was unlikely to even be able to be a pilot, but at that time, my dreams had been taken away. From there, I started down a career path of engineering and management that turned out quite well for me, but at that time, I was just stumbling along with no real idea where I might end up.

After Lori graduated, she decided, with quite a bit of pressure from her parents, that she would attend a college on the other side of Michigan. I was surprised and hurt that she, after telling me she wouldn't wait for me if I joined the air force, had decided to move away for college. Never mind that she could come home most weekends and we were always only a phone call away; I used this perceived slight as a way to justify my first infidelity.

As I entered into a relationship with Kylie (names of my girlfriends have been changed for privacy reasons), a girl I had known and been friends with from high school, the relationship escalated to the point that it ended up in us sharing a bed. Selfishly, and unreasonably, I justified that if Lori had truly cared about me, she would not have gone away to school. I developed my relationship with Kylie. Also, my pride was likely boosted by the fact that another woman had found me attractive. I was able to focus all of my attention on me and what I needed and wanted to be happy and not consider the pain I was inflicting on someone else. I was twenty years old at that time but had the self-confidence of a small child. The lack of self-esteem I had from the fact that both of my fathers had left me put a deep need inside me to please others and crave attention and praise. When another girl had started to show me attention and found me attractive, it fed all the things inside me that needed and craved this attention.

The new relationship ended somewhat quickly after we recognized it for what it was. I enjoyed spending time with my new friend and found her funny, attractive, and interesting, but I think we both realized that what we had shared was not going to last. I also quickly realized after we had slept together what I had done and felt instant remorse. I didn't wait long to tell Lori about what had happened, and she was understandably devastated. We had grown up together, had shared everything together, and had made future plans for the rest of our lives together. I had selfishly ripped those dreams away from her by thinking about myself and my desires and not keeping her in my heart. I realize now that if one truly keeps God at the center of their relationship, it is really difficult to even consider being unfaithful. If you spend regular time with God in prayer and share this with your spouse, you know that you are not only being unfaithful to your partner if you cheat, but you are breaking an oath to God as well.

The utter pain that I saw Lori exhibit, the breathlessness and the unbelief is something I will never forget. I will never forget it because, unbelievably, and for a time unforgivably, it was not the only time that I put her through this pain. I know many people say that once a cheater, always a cheater. I disagree. I will say, once a cheater, always a cheater unless you descend fully, hit your rock bottom, and do the work to begin to ascend. Just as a drug abuser or alcoholic can do inexplicable things that hurt others to the point that their family disowns them, people that are unfaithful harm others through their own addictions and personal shortcomings. Recovery is possible, but like any twelve-step program, one must have a higher power and go through much pain to get onto and stay on the road to recovery.

After much discussion, time away from each other, and the thought of losing each other, Lori and I reconciled. We had become so codependent upon each other at this point, no matter what we did to each other, we were not going to let each other go and move on. I felt true remorse for the choices I had made and promised that it would never happen again if only she would give me another chance. I would prove that I would and could love her and we would live happily ever after. After all, we had promised each other that if we got married, we would never divorce each other and put our children through what we had gone through.

After reconciling and dealing with her parents who had found out about my choices, we got married later the next year. I know in my heart I loved her as much as my heart could love at that time. I did not enter into the marriage considering ever being unfaithful again. I was happy to have a second chance and knew I could only be happy with her. This idea that I need and must have a relationship with a specific person to be happy, that I could not possibly be happy without her, was a clear sign that I was lacking in my own love for myself at that time. When I say clear sign, I mean that it is clear to me now after more than thirty years of pain, struggles, climbing back up, and really giving myself over to a higher power. At that time, it just seemed that this head-over-heels love for each other was what real love looked like. Neither my wife nor I had any good adult role models of a healthy relationship to model our marriage after. Much as we learned to raise our children on our own, we learned how to try to make a marriage work on our own with no real gold standard to pattern our nuptials on.

Seven years later, after white-knuckling the first half decade or so of our marriage, I fell off the fidelity wagon again. They say an alcoholic on a desert island is not really a recovered alcoholic; he just doesn't have anything to drink, so he is dry. Similarly, I had not worked through the root cause of my desire and need to be unfaithful, so though I was faithful for the first seven years of our marriage, it was out of pure willpower, and the thoughts of being with other women would often come back. At that time, I would justify them in any number of ways. My wife was not an overly sexual person, not like the women I had seen on the sex scenes I had seen on so many movies. Thus, I selfishly justified, she was not treating me the way a man deserved to be treated even though I was working really hard at work and making good money and helping with the kids around the house. All excuses to justify my behavior, but at that time, they seemed to be justifiable, and the sleight felt real. As my career took off and I started traveling for work, I had the opportunity to be in the wrong place at the wrong time on many occasions. Like the man who hasn't had a drink in years and is then rescued from the desert island only to find himself on a yacht with a stocked bar, I had travels that opened the liquor cabinet of temptation for me as well.

Being a project manager for a global company and living across the country from my family was the start of my downfall. I would live onsite for a week or two at a time and then fly home for a weekend. I would call home each night and talk to my wife and the kids, but it was fifteen to thirty minutes of trying to be present, while all the while knowing fun and adventure waited just outside the door for me. I had a company credit card, so every meal was at a local bar or restaurant, and it didn't take long for me to become close friends with one of the women, Patricia, who worked there. Like every new relationship, it seemed fresh and wonderful, and this new person seemed so interesting and so much more fun. And why wouldn't she? None of the real-world responsibilities of raising children, paying bills, working through relationship issues were present in this new relationship. These affairs were based upon fantasy and were an escape for me. Again, the hole deep inside of me that craved attention and praise and love had never been filled. This is not a hole that someone else can pour their love into and fill up. This is a hole deep inside that can only be filled with self-love and love of God. When we look to others to fill this hole in our soul, through words of praise and affirmation or sexual relationships, we will always be left wanting. Additionally, until we fill that hole in ourselves with self-love, we cannot truly and deeply love another. The old saying of "you cannot give what you do not have" is absolutely true.

As this relationship escalated, again, I told my wife that I was having feelings for someone else. She quickly called bullshit and knew

I had crossed the line again and been unfaithful. Again, I looked on in absolute self-loathing as I saw this good and decent woman who had given me a second chance have her heart torn out again. Sadly, I think that she too lacked this important love of self. This self-love is not to be confused with egotism or escalation of self over others. It is simply a love of oneself and knowledge of God's ever-present and eternal love for our self that our ultimate happiness is not contingent upon another's love. This is not to say that we are not devasted by the news of an unfaithful spouse, but that we have the love of ourselves that we can walk away from the relationship knowing that it is toxic and hurtful, whether intended or not.

After this episode in our relationship, we did take time away from each other. My wife had a brief relationship with another man she had met through friends. I had ended the relationship with my new girlfriend, Patricia, when it became clear I would have to choose between her and my children. She was not prepared to move across country and be away from her family, and I was not prepared to move away from my children to be with her. Of course, selfishly, we had never discussed this when we were developing our relationship. What did we think the long-term outcome would be? Our eyes were clouded with the new relationship fog that so easily makes it difficult to see beyond the next time you will see each other.

My wife and I filed for divorce during this time as we were sure our marriage was done. After going through this again, I was sure that she wasn't going to make me happy, and she was sure she did not want to trust or get hurt again by someone who claimed to love her and yet put her through so much pain.

In Michigan at that time, and perhaps other states as well, once you file for divorce, there was a six-month waiting period for the divorce to be final. I thought, at that time, how stupid and useless. I just wanted to move on from this relationship, never mind that my heart was broken for not keeping the promise I had made to myself for my children that I would never put them through a divorce like I had gone through as a child.

My wife and I continued to stay in touch as necessary to work through the divorce requirements such as who would get the stuff that we had acquired. That seemed like such an important issue at that time. We discussed who would see the kids on what days and all the other items that had to be worked out. All the time, we kept talking about why this had happened and who was to blame. In my shame and embarrassment, I blamed her for not being a good wife. She blamed me, rightfully so, for not keeping my promise to her. That promise to her was in fact part of the issue. I had made a promise to her alone on that wedding day to be faithful. I had not made a sacramental oath to God that comes along with a real marriage. I fully understand that there are committed and faithful relationships that are joined legally in a courthouse with no reference to a covenantal oath to God to be faithful, but for me and my faith upbringing and my shortcomings, this promise to another person was, sadly, easily breakable due to my own deficiencies.

As the six-month period was coming to a close, my wife and I had a meeting at our house that she and the kids had been living in. We had become less angry with each other over the course of the six months and amazingly realized we missed each other. Having known each other for over ten years at that point, she, to my utter surprise, asked if I thought we might try to work it out and stay together. I was taken aback but almost immediately said yes, I would very much love and appreciate that opportunity. I had learned my lesson and had missed her and the kids and was beyond grateful for another opportunity to have my family back and make good on my promise to my children to not put them through a divorce. It was a happy time for me, even though I once again had to face her family again. I am not sure that they ever understood why she would give me yet another chance after causing her so much pain. I don't think they realized how lacking we both were in so many ways and how together we found what we were lacking in ourselves.

Once again, I was back on the desert island, free from temptations of that first drink and able to focus on just making the best of things. Again, I felt a deep debt to my wife for allowing me the chance to have my family back and tried to travel less. We had started going to church a bit more, but it was really not a deep and committed relationship to God. We would pretty much try to go every Sunday, but once we walked out the doors after mass, we didn't really talk too much about God again until it was time to go to church again the following week. The seed of the Gospel we heard each Sunday, for me anyways, was falling on rocky ground, "Where it did not have much soil, and immediately it sprang up, since it had no depth of soil. And when the sun rose, it was scorched and since it had no root, it withered away" (Mark 4: 3-9).

We continued our relationship over the next fifteen years. There were times of great struggles and also times of great happiness. Mostly, the happiness was surrounded by events associated with our sons—seeing them do well in school, watching them succeed in sporting events, and making new friends and all the things that parents are proud of. This is not to minimize the relationship with my wife. Like all relationships I was aware of at that time, there were just ups and downs where we grew closer and farther apart and then back together. Our lives had really stopped being about each other and our relationship and were really about supporting and teaching the children.

It is with some remorse and regret that I see now that the greatest lesson I could have shown my sons is how important it is not only to be a great father but also be a great husband. So often to be a fun dad, I would make Lori the butt of jokes that my kids found funny but diminished her for the sake of our laughter. It was just a joke I would justify, but any joke that demeans and hurts another to get a laugh is not one that should be told. After a while, I think my wife would laugh along with the jokes so as not to seem like she had no sense of humor, but in the end, it was teaching my sons a bad example of getting laughter at the expense of another. That the other was their mom was worse yet.

My final failure as a husband came fifteen years or so after we had reconciled and gotten back together. My sons were finishing high school and were preparing to enter college, and the thought of just my wife and me alone in the house became a reality we had not thought of in a long time. Our relationship had gotten less and less intimate, and we had grown farther apart in our interests. Beside the boys, there were few things we shared in common. I loved sports, as did the boys, and when they took to playing sports in high school, I got fully engaged. My youngest son was very driven by the sport of wrestling and began to really excel in it. I volunteered to help and spent a great deal of time with my youngest son participating in this sport. I also started to work out a lot and get into much better shape. At this point, I had also started to drink on a fairly regular basis. I had never drunk when the boys were young and in fact never had my first drink until I was twenty-seven years old. After that point, I did not drink in front of the boys, and it was not until high school that they even knew that I drank.

As I grew more confident in myself and my pride swelled with compliments, I again lost focus on my promises and instead turned it toward other women. It might be safe to think that someone in their forties would have worked through their childhood issues and their lack of self-worth. That would be untrue as it relates to me, and I suspect many others. These issues and struggles we develop as children do not simply disappear when we hit a magic age. We can carry them with us to our graves if we don't decide to admit we have an issue and begin to do the work on it. I was so easily swayed by simple compliments, and again, when they were coming from a beautiful woman, I was so easily affected. Again, when my wife went away to visit friends, I used the opportunity of her selfishness in thinking of herself, which was a total fabrication on my part, to justify my actions. If she was going to think and take care of herself, I would do the same for me. We didn't really love each other anymore, I told myself. We didn't have anything in common, and if other women found me attractive and wanted to pay me attention, I was all too willing to accept it. It is unfair to say that I saw these other women in my life as simply something to satisfy my desires. I felt each time that I was truly in love with them. Again, that new relationship fog makes each one seem as if they were the most interesting and amazing person and how lucky I was that they had taken an interest in me. The affairs of the heart that I had experienced were truly that, I fell deeply in love, or perhaps infatuation is a better word, with this new relationship.

When my wife came home, I told her that I was tired of always fighting and not doing the things together and didn't enjoy being married. She asked if I wanted to get a divorce, or perhaps she even said maybe we should get divorced, and I immediately said I thought that was a good idea. After all, she had suggested it, not me, so that made it somehow better and more justifiable in my mind. I had not let my children down; their mom had asked for the divorce. Total bullshit, I know, but for a drowning man, any life preserver seems like a good idea, even if the one thrown to you will actually pull you to the bottom.

So, after twenty-two years of being married and twenty-five years of being together, we finally realized our relationship was not healthy and got divorced. The fact that the final women that I had an affair with was friends with my wife made it even more painful and embarrassing for my wife. Though we had had plenty of good times together over the twenty-five years together, there was no amount of happiness that could make up for the pain I had caused in our relationship. I felt, again, overwhelming remorse for the choices I had made. I was living a fantasy life with my new girlfriend, whom I cared deeply about and actually proposed to before we separated but was so sorry about how I had treated my wife. Many "friends" I had made at the bar during this time justified it by saying I deserved more and deserved better and it was time to move on and that my wife and I didn't seem right together and on and on.

Looking in the Mirror

There is a saying that when we are at our best, we are like mirrors that reflect God's love and holiness. Like a mirror, the reflection can be overwhelmingly bright when it reflects the sun, but when covered with dirt, any reflection of light is not possible.

Perhaps the hardest part of my perceiving my ascent while actually descending was the deep reflection it caused me to have and the pain it caused my children and other loved ones. I still recall, almost ten years later, the pain and shame I felt when one of my sons had to step out of a school event because he was overwhelmed with sadness that his mom and dad were getting divorced. I rationalized it away at the time by saying he was almost out of high school and kids are resilient and divorces happen all the time, basically anything that would make myself feel better for putting those whom I loved into such pain.

When the separation started to take place in earnest, I had to move out of the family house. I could have fought for it and argued about who got what, but I think my sense of guilt and shame really made me want to try to salvage some good out of the event. I stated that I would leave the house to my wife and would cover the payments through spousal and child support. When the day came to move out of the family house and into the new apartment, everything I owned, everything I said I would take with me, fit into the back of a pickup truck. Here I was in my early forties having worked hard for the last twenty-five years and through the result of my own choices, everything I owed fit into the four-foot-by-eight-foot area of the back of a pickup truck.

After the initial "woe is me" attitude, I felt a strangely freeing feeling from the loss of most of my material goods. Though I was still in the midst of this significant event in my life, I saw that the lack of material possessions was not necessarily a bad thing. Sure, I was a bit embarrassed at the time that I had worked my whole life and now really didn't own very much, but I also didn't have much to lose at that point. I saw the first glimpses of a life without material possessions driving me and the freedom it allowed. At that point, what I did with the freedom was continue to spiral deeper into my descent through drinking and finding satisfaction through others.

As a truly good parent who never gives up on their child, God waited patiently for me to learn from my mistakes and listen to His advice. I continued to develop a relationship with my girlfriend Judy during this time after my divorce and truly saw the damaging repercussions of alcoholism. Throughout this new relationship, I experienced many things that would eventually help me to get back on path God had intended for me. One of the most humbling experiences during this time was when Judy put me through the pain I had put my ex-wife through so many times by having a relationship with another person. I suddenly felt the pain, the shame, the humiliation of being on the other end of these choices. Though we tried to reconcile a number of times, the pain this breach of faith caused between us was not something we could recover from, and we eventually ended up splitting up. Through all of this, because of the issues with my new girlfriend and her journey to deepen her faith, I had finally turned the corner and recognized that only through a real and living relationship with God would I ever find the happiness that He has promised for us.

CHAPTER 9
The Journey Back

If patience is worth anything, it must endure to the end of time. And a living faith will last in the midst of the blackest storm.
—Mahatma Gandhi

A Real and Deepened Faith

God is rumored to work in mysterious ways. None would be more mysterious than how he allowed me to find grace in the midst of my culmination of poor choices. When I had entered into the relationship with Judy, my new girlfriend after my divorce, we felt what we thought was a true love for each other, and with that came the desire for a lifetime together. Though that was not to be the case; at that time, we felt we wanted to take the steps that we believed would enable this. Through the grace of God, Judy decided that she would like to join the Catholic faith to share that with me. Through the separation and eventual divorce with my wife, I had started to lean on my faith more, and Judy felt that she too would like to experience and share this.

With the Catholic faith, it's not so easy to just walk in the front door of the church and announce to the priest that you wanted to be Catholic, and bang, you are made a Catholic in good standing. To join the faith, as an adult, one must take RCIA classes. The Rite of Christian Initiation for Adults classes are designed to teach the applicant about the faith over a longer period, usually nine months or so, and then culminating on Easter vigil mass, the applicant receives any sacraments that they may not have had yet, and they are allowed to enter the Catholic faith as full members. To experience a full Easter vigil mass and see both youths and adults receive the sacraments of baptism and first communion has always been an awe-inspiring event for me. The mass itself is several hours long. The priest may start by lighting a fire outside the church and bringing the flame into the darkened church where it is shared with all community members who have small candles. The entire church is illuminated with nothing but the light of hundreds of small candles. It is a powerful experience and one I look forward to each year.

When a person enters this RCIA program, they are required to have a sponsor. This sponsor is an active Catholic who can help them with their questions and give them guidance over the nine months as they learn and grow their faith. As a way to strengthen our relationship, I volunteered to sponsor Judy in her journey and promised to share my knowledge of the faith with her. Little did I know at that time how much I would learn and how little I actually knew about my own faith. So many times, I would be asked by her why the church teaches this or why it does this during mass, and so many times I had to respond, "That's just how we do it. I don't know why." I had always just accepted the routines and rituals of the church at face value and never dug deeper into why. I was skimming along on the surface of the faith not knowing or really looking to see how deep the waters went. Through my experience as a sponsor, I not only wondered how deep the waters went, but I jumped off the boat into the ocean of God's love and started to see how vastly deep this faith went. So deep I couldn't come close to seeing the bottom, and that scared me.

Fortunately for me, Susan, the RCIA director at the church we were going to at that time, the church I had went to every weekend with my wife and family for the last ten years, was a very spiritual and committed Catholic woman. In my life, I have always connected closely and been attentive to direction from many wise women in my life. It started with my grandmother and carried on through so many other amazing women God had put in my life. It was a blessing for me that this director had just graduated from the seminary and could answer any question Judy and I had and did so in a way that was never demeaning. There was never any, "You've been a Catholic for forty years, and you don't know this" sort of vibe. It always seemed to me she was happy and joyful to share her knowledge of the faith with us.

We completed the RCIA program in the spring of that year, perhaps 2011; my girlfriend Judy attended Easter vigil and was baptized and became a member of the Catholic church. Though we would end up separating later that year, it was a powerful experience for me to be part of her faith journey. Through the classes, I asked our director Susan many questions about our faith and also about the seminary. It was my understanding that seminaries were closed institutions that taught celibate young men how to become Roman Catholic priests. As Susan was married, I assumed she was neither celibate nor a young man, so I was not sure how she was allowed to go to a seminary. She patiently talked to me about all of questions and let me know that yes, lay people, those in the church who are not part of the clergy, can attend seminary and actually study right alongside the men who are in formation for priesthood.

Sacred Heart Major Seminary in Detroit, Michigan, was the seminary that I attended that changed the course of my life. Founded in 1919 by Bishop Michael Gallagher, Sacred Heart has been the cornerstone of Catholic higher education in Detroit for over a century. When I attended, there were approximately 100 seminarians in residence at the seminary and about 350 lay students like myself. Many of the lay students were older men and women who were attending after their day jobs to get an education in theology, pastoral studies, and various other degrees for any number of reasons. The staff at Sacred Heart is made up of amazing professors who really took time to educate me on the basics of my faith all the way through to the more complicated aspects. I think my faith was set on fire as well because of the opportunity to attend classes with so many of the young seminarians. To see these young men, barely older or in some cases younger than my own sons, on fire with their faith so passionately that they were dedicating their lives to it really inspired me. I was in an environment where I could talk openly about my faith and my beliefs and not worry about offending anyone. I could ask questions, so many questions, about what I did not understand about Catholicism and find out that many others had that were catechized the same time I was had many of the same questions.

Like any major political movement, faith, or other large gathering of people, there are different perspectives on the Catholic faith. There are Catholics that are more liberal that interpret scripture to mean one thing and put the focus on Jesus's teaching on certain aspects. Conversely, there are conservative Catholics that interpret scripture to mean something slightly different and focus on other aspects of Jesus's teaching. Growing up in a liberal environment, I realized it was helpful to my growth that the majority of the professors at the seminary were fairly strict and conservative in their beliefs and their teachings. It helped me to grow and see another side of my faith that I had not seen and to understand why the church taught what it taught.

Like a child who has discovered something new, I was enthralled with the new knowledge I was learning and openly shared my new knowledge with anyone that was interested and often with those that were not. I had started to learn things that a lot of the faithful in the parish pews next to me each Sunday did not know, and truth be told, I think I was pompously arrogant with my new knowledge. Knowing that I had the "truth," I was ever so anxious to educate and share it with others, likely to show how smart and faithful I had become. Luckily, I had entered into a new relationship a year or so after separating from Judy, and my new girlfriend, Tami, was never shy about questioning my new knowledge and making me really dig even deeper into my faith.

I had entered the seminary at first just to take a few classes and see what it was all about, and I very quickly fell in love with the place and couldn't wait to take more classes. I chose a MAPS degree, masters in pastoral studies, with an emphasis on health care as my major. I had discerned that perhaps my long-term goal was to become a hospital or hospice chaplain, and this was a good degree to help me along the way. I knew this was going to be a few years down the road as I still had financial obligations from my divorce and financial help for my college age children, but it was a good long-term goal. I was in classes with several like-minded individuals, and the time at the seminary seemed like and oasis of calm in my otherwise hectic day. In particular, the chapel at the seminary is a sacred and holy place and where I spent many, many hours in prayer. Often after work, I would leave early just to get to the chapel an hour or so before class so I could say my rosary in front of the Our Lady of Guadalupe shrine and have some quiet time for meditation to calm my mind. The chapel is a cavernous facility in which the lighting is often provided by just a few candles around the facility. In the middle of Detroit, it is remarkably quiet and serene at the seminary in general and the chapel especially. I felt a sense of calm, of peace, and of love that I had not experienced prior to that. I felt God present in the woodwork and the walls of the chapel, and his love and forgiveness seeped into my very skin as I sat in the quiet darkness and listened for his voice.

Scripture—The Word of God

Perhaps the most enduring and impactful habit I picked up from my time in the seminary was the love of reading scripture. Growing up a Catholic in the seventies and eighties, I never, I mean never, picked up a Bible and read from scripture. I would listen intently, more or less, in mass on Sunday, and I am sure we had a Bible around the house somewhere, but daily reading of scripture was not something that I or anyone in my family ever did. When I heard it in church, I had not studied or reflected on it and often, especially Old Testament verses, which seemed like they were completely unintelligible, and I didn't understand at all how those could be the words of God and what they meant to me. I didn't really care too much about all the lineages that were described so often in the Old Testament, and while I knew the stories well, I could not recite scripture and tell you from which book or chapter it was from.

That all changed pretty quickly once I entered the seminary. As you can probably guess, not surprisingly, the backbone of everything taught at the seminary is based upon scripture. As the divinely inspired word of God, scripture is the playbook for the game of life for Christians. Similar to how Muslims have the Holy Koran and Hindus have the Gita and Upanishads, Christians have the Holy Bible. Several of my first courses were devoted specifically to scripture with specific classes on the Old and New testament and on the Gospels. I really found the class on the Old Testament infinitely useful and eye-opening for me. I was blessed to have Dr. Mary Healy as a professor. Dr. Healy had a gift of making the difficult understandable and for explaining what all those cryptic verses in the Old Testament really meant. I started to get an understanding for scripture like I had never had before, and it totally opened my eyes and my mind. It was like a light had been turned on that had been kept dark for forty years. All the questions that I had wondered about since I was a child began to be answered without me even asking them. If our life is a puzzle with so many pieces scattered across a table, I finally started to see the big picture and was able to slowly and sometimes painfully start to find pieces that fit together. That same sense of joy that you get when you search for a missing puzzle piece and incorrectly try several pieces that don't quite fit, and then find the right one and a bigger picture starts to take shape, that was what was happening to me with my faith.

Sr. Mary—A Voice of Compassion

In the midst of all this light being shown upon me, I was overwhelmed with knowledge but perhaps lacking a bit in loving wisdom. I was learning the theology, and for that I was grateful, but I was wielding it a bit like a sword. Instead of using the knowledge and love I was learning about as a soothing balm to help the pain I was seeing in the world, I was using it as a sword to defend my knowledge. I was learning about a God of love, but not how to love.

One class turned me around on my foundation and brought me back down to the ground. Sr. Mary had been an institution within the institution for over fifty years. Starting in 1969, Sr. Mary taught thousands of seminarians and lay students. She was a voice in the darkness when many around her wanted to silence her about the need for social justice for the neediest in society. Sr. Mary taught a required course called Sacred Scripture. It was a run-through of the entire Old and New testament in one semester. It was one of the first classes we were required to take, and it opened up the mind of us students, at least me anyway, to seeing scripture in different light. Instead of a harsh and judgmental God, I experienced a loving and caring God who sought to know me personally and love and forgive me personally for what I had done.

I recall just weeks into the class thinking I had developed a special relationship with Sr. Mary as she was so very caring and radiated love. I talked to my fellow students, men and women alike, and found that they also felt that they had developed this special bond with her. It seemed as if everyone she met was best friends with her. Over a private lunch in the cafeteria, I shared my story with her. I shared how my thoughts of my Muslim friends I had made in Egypt while traveling as righteous and holy men. Despite our differences in beliefs, it did not quite square up with some of the lessons I was being taught in the seminary. This line of discussion really caught her interest, and she asked me if I would my mind doing her a favor. Would I bring my dishdasha that I had been given while in Egypt and put it on during class? At first apprehensive, she assured it would be a good teaching moment. I agreed and brought it into class the next week. At a certain time in class, when talking about religious garb of different faiths, she nodded to me and told the class that I had an example of religious garb to share and asked what everyone thought of it after I put it on. I shared my story of my friend Mohamed traveling to Mecca for Hajj and how he had purchased this garment for me in Mecca and given it to me as a sign of friendship. There were mixed emotions and ideas about me wearing a long white Arabic dishdasha, but it sparked exactly the conversation that Sr. Mary had wanted to have. We openly discussed preconceived notions of other faiths based upon what we saw and read and discussed further what we could learn and appreciate from each other. I recall this incident clearly and was glad I was able to help in this teaching moment by sharing something so personal to me.

It was through Sr. Mary's class that I also learned firsthand about social justice and a loving, caring, and forgiving God. She would share stories with us about her religious orders, the Home Visitors of Mary, vocations. She talked about their call to help people in the inner city. Sr. Mary shared many stories of encounters with homeless people in Detroit and how she saw Jesus in them and helped me to understand how to try to see Jesus in everyone I meet. It was through her tutelage and guidance that the idea that I was called for hospice care and chaplaincy first came to me. At first, her suggestion that I would be gifted in working with elderly people and those on hospice care seemed completely out of left field. I felt awkward around older people I didn't know and certainly didn't feel I was able to participate in any sort of pastoral care. After all, I was just really learning about my faith, and I was deathly afraid someone would ask me a question I could not answer, and I would be figured out as a fraud. Three years and dozens of hospice patients later, I found that what Sr. Mary had seen in me was that God had given me a gift to listen and care for those in difficult times. She had seen in me what I could not see in myself and had given me the courage to start down a new path that I would not have taken without her gentle nudging.

Sr. Mary did not limit her instructions to pie-in-the-sky ideals but provided useful help for issues I was dealing with. While I had her for just the one class, I maintained a relationship with her for the duration of my years at the seminary, and we would meet once or twice a year and have lunch in the cafeteria and catch up. We would also meet if I felt I really needed to talk to her about something. She was clear that she did not have the time to devote to be my spiritual director but always seemed to make time for a talk. During my first year at the seminary, a very troubling issue had happened to a young lady whom I cared for very much. She was just a teenager and the daughter of my friend, but I loved her like my own daughter. I had seen her grow up from just a toddler and was very proud of the young lady she was becoming. I found out that she had attended a party and had been given some drugs and had been taken advantage of by a young man in the community. I was so angry and full of hatred toward him; I truly wanted to find this young man and make him pay for what he had done to my friend's daughter. I could hardly sleep at night because of the anger and sadness of the injustice of the situation. I came to Sr. Mary with this and asked her how in the world I could ever forgive someone for doing this to someone I loved very much. Calmly, she talked to me about different examples of Jesus loving the person but disliking the actions. Then she gave me some advice that released me from the prison of my anger. Take the boy's name that had done this, write it down on a piece of paper, and put it next to my bed. Before going to sleep, take the slip of paper and say his name and pray to God for him. She knew it would not be possible over time for me to hate someone that I was praying for. As distasteful and impossible as this sounded, to pray for someone who had so greatly wronged someone I cared for, I followed her advice. In less than a week, the hatred for the person had gone from my heart. My anger at his actions remained, but the chains of hatred that had bound my heart had been broken by God, and my heart was free to love again.

To this day, I recall this practical example of how to love in the most difficult of times and thank Sr. Mary for truly teaching me what it means in the Bible in Matthew 22:34-40 when,

> Jesus said unto him, Thou shalt love the Lord thy God with all thy heart, and with all thy soul, and with all thy mind. This is the first and great commandment. And the second is like unto it, thou shalt love thy neighbor as thyself. On these two commandments hang all the law and the prophets. (Matthew 22:37-40)

Another amazing gift that Sr. Mary gave to me was the practice of extended Lectio Divina. Lectio Divina is the practice of Sacred Reading and is a hallmark of Benedictine Spirituality. In our Benedictine oblate meetings, we would often practice Lectio Divina. Brother Mark from the Benedictine Monastery in Michigan would read a small section of scripture, usually from the Gospel for the following Sunday, never the entire Gospel reading, but just a line or two or three at the most. He would reread the section numerous times with prayerful silence between each reading. After that, he would ask if anyone had a message to share after reflecting deeply on a certain word or phrase from the reading of these few lines. It was amazing how God spoke to each person who felt like sharing during this time. This practice is a way to dig deeper into the Gospel. Sr. Mary introduced an extended Lectio practice to me while at the seminary. In this practice, each Monday, you find the Gospel reading for the following Sunday and slowly read and reflect on it. Maybe read it a few times. After that, each day of the week, I would reread the Gospel and see what message came to me throughout the week. It was amazing how the Gospel came alive and lived and changed throughout the week for me when I utilized this practice. In the past, I would hear the Gospel on Sunday for the first time when it was read in church that day. Now, I had lived with this Gospel all week and was well prepared for it when it was read in mass on Sunday. In addition to this extended Lectio, I began to use a book from St. Thomas Aquinas entitled the *Catena Aurea*. The name is Latin for "The Golden Chain," and what a chain it was. Aquinas had collected lectures and homilies from the doctors of the church and the saints and put them into one book and categorized them by each reading in the Gospel. So, for example, if the Sunday

Gospel was the ever popular John 3:16, instead of just thinking of a dude with a rainbow-colored afro holding up a John 3:16 sign in the end zone of a football game, I could look in the *Catena Aurea* and see what the greatest minds in church history interpreted this to mean. It was amazing how this practice opened up the Gospel even further for me. I would reflect on my own on the Gospel, but then going further and seeing what all these brilliant minds thought of this Gospel opened up so many new roads of thought for me. For all this deeper appreciation of the Gospel, I have Sr. Mary to thank for these new tools she had given me.

Third Orders

Along with seminarians who were studying to be diocesan priests, the ones you see in Church each weekend and lay students like me, there were also others who attended classes at the seminary with me. These men, they were only men, came dressed in brown or blue robes, with rosary-type beads as a belt around their waist. Who were these Jedi-looking fellows and did they in fact carry light sabers? I was not really sure who these guys were and what their manner of dress represented.

After waiting a few weeks to ask someone, because I was sure everyone knew but me and I felt silly asking, after all, I should have known who these guys were, I summoned the courage to ask someone who they were. "Oh, those guys, those are brothers of a monastic order, and they are going to be ordained priests for their community" was the almost intelligible response I got. Monastic orders? Community? While that helped a bit, I realized I was going to have to spend a little time with Google to get to the root of this question.

It was after studying about monasticism at home that I learned that monks were not relegated to the annals of history in the middle ages; there were still monks living among us. I learned of different orders within the Catholic faith, names I may have vaguely heard about such as Franciscans, Benedictines, Dominicans, Jesuits, and other names straight out of the stories of Robin Hood and the renaissance period. I learned that each of the different orders had different charisms, different gifts from God that their order stressed. For Benedictines, it was in trying to live their lives according to the Gospels as well as the Rule of St. Benedict that their charism for contemplative prayer and work expressed itself. Franciscans, named after, you probably can guess, St. Francis, were known as those who lived their lives according to the Gospel and were active and spreading this faith through various activities. Dominicans, named after St. Dominic and identified by an "OP" (Order of Preacher) after their name, are known for sharing the word of God through their preaching. All of these labels are severely limiting of the full grace that each order shares with the world but helps to identify the gifts they bring.

As I was growing deeper and deeper in my faith through my studies at the seminary and my relationship with my girlfriend Tami, she challenged me daily to put the teachings I had learned in the classroom into practical use that mirrored the teachings of Jesus, and I became more interested in these monastic orders. Through speaking with colleagues at the seminary and the monastic brothers themselves, I learned about a publication entitled *Vision Vocations Guide*. This publication shares information on all of the different monastic orders and gives contact information for each along with descriptions of what life in this order might look like. This was an invaluable resource for me as I sought to learn more about these mysterious individuals. I had so many questions. How did these brothers find out about these orders? What was it like to live in community? Did they have to wear any clothes under their robes? Did they wear sandals even when there was two feet of snow on the ground (I found out the answer was yes to this last question as I watched the brothers jump through the snow with nothing but Birkenstocks on their feet)?

As I spoke to them before and after class and as I flipped through the pages of *Vision Vocation Guide*, I learned about something called a third order or a tertiary order. These third orders allowed lay people such as me to more closely associate themselves with specific monastic orders and communities. I quickly looked up resources on the Internet to see if there were any active third order groups in my area. To my surprise, I found out that there were Franciscan and Benedictine groups within an hour of my house. I looked for a Jesuit third order as I was interested in the teaching and adventurous spirit of the Jesuits I had read about, this was before Pope Francis, a Jesuit, was elected to be pope. To my disappointment, I learned that Jesuits do not have a third order similar to other orders. After striking out there, I sent an e-mail to the Franciscan group near me. I patiently and virtuously waited for a reply. I waited and waited, and after not hearing anything, I sent another e-mail to see if the first had gotten through. Again, under the watchful eye of God, I waited for this door to open to allow me to step further into my faith. Again, the door remained locked as no reply was ever sent. Finally, running out of options and already down two strikes in the count, I sent an e-mail to the oblate director at St. Benedict Monastery in Oxford, Michigan. Crack, I had made contact and lined a solid single into left field. The director responded within a few days, which I later learned was a very quick response from him, and asked that we talk or meet to discuss this further.

After our initial meeting for me to see if this seemed like something God was calling me to and for the director to see if I was someone who he felt had this charism, we decided this was a relationship worth developing, and I began my novitiate year with the Benedictine monastery in Oxford, Michigan. I was on my third strike and was happy to find this opportunity. Little did I know how fortuitous this relationship would end up being for my future wife and I and how God had guided me even when I clearly did not understand what my charism was and which direction I should go. The Benedictine order and its goal to balance prayer and work, *Ora et Labora* in Latin, would end up being exactly what I needed in my life when I was ready for it.

Diocesan Life

As I progressed in my studies at the seminary and got closer to attaining my degree in pastoral studies, I was required to have a formal spiritual director. While I had many people guiding me and giving me informal direction, it was not the same as having a dedicated spiritual director whom I would talk to on a regular basis. I did not really understand the criteria for selecting a spiritual director so didn't really know where to start. So, having started to develop a friendly relationship with our local parish priest, I asked him if he could recommend a spiritual director for me. Having recently graduated from the seminary himself and being a spiritual director for several seminarians, which I was not aware of, he kindly volunteered that he could provide spiritual direction for me.

A spiritual director meets with the directee on a regular basis. It can be every week, every month, or whatever is deemed appropriate after getting to know each other. The director's goal is not so much to tell the directee what they should do but to help guide them to discover what God is asking of them and what their path might be. It is not a counselor who listens to your issues and tells you what to do. Instead, in my experience, a good spiritual director listens to where you are on your journey, tries to understand what you think your path is, and then asks questions and provides insight to help you along the way. As one grows deeper in their faith and new things come to light, things one may not be familiar with, a spiritual director in invaluable to gently shepherd us toward the greener pastures.

I was learning so much at this point in my life about my faith, my relationships, the mistakes I had made in my life, and my guilt and remorse for those I had hurt, I wondered what God's plan was for me, how He could forgive me (hint, He already had), and how He could love me again (hint, He never stopped loving me). Having a spiritual director to share these faith and personal-based questions with was an invaluable tool to help me in my growth. I was so blessed to have such a kind and caring individual to take me under his wing and guide me along the path.

As my faith grew and my spiritual direction happened on a more regular basis, I became more involved with the innerworkings of the local parish. The parish was a small church in the small town in which I had grown up in. It was the church I had attended for a good portion of my childhood, and it held many memories for me such as attending mass with my mother and grandmother and seeing the kids I didn't like in school sitting just a few pews over from me. As part of a diocesan program to help with tuition assistance, there was a grant, I think it was called the Fisherman's fund, in reference to Jesus's statement to Peter that He would make him a fisher of men. Part of the stipulation of me receiving this small amount of tuition assistance, any amount was helpful, was that I had to participate and help out at a parish located in the archdiocese of Detroit. I was more than happy to help in whatever way my schedule allowed as my parish priest was a kind and generous man, and I was happy to help him to take some of the load off.

What I learned, as I got more involved, was the tremendous workload that parish priests are under. I know that Jesus said that His yoke is easy, and His burden is light, but that may have been before the drastic priest shortage that the United States is experiencing in the twenty-first century. Priests are pretty much on call 24/7. Things like deaths, marriages, baptisms, anointing of the sick, regular daily masses, and so many other things from running a parish to maintaining faithfulness to the Liturgy of the Hours they are required to recite daily, priests are being boiled alive in a pressure cooker of expectations. Add to that pressure the stigma of the Catholic priest from the sex abuse crisis, and it is amazing to me that so many young men accept the call of the Lord to join the priesthood when it is such a demanding job. Every priest I know that has accepted this call has done it out of a sincere love of God and desire to be His voice and His shepherd here on earth. These young men are called upon to give selflessly of themselves, to remain celibate, and to give their body and soul for the good of their church and their parishioners. Amazingly, so many do this gladly, happily as their vocation in life calls for. Even more surprising, I know many are filled with joy and love for this vocation and cannot seriously imagine doing anything else.

I quickly found out that, even though I was not asked to be one, I did not have the vocation of a diocesan priest. After sitting through church council meetings where church members, those that claimed to be good God-fearing and Christ-loving Christians went at each other with such vitriol that they often threw their books down and stormed out of the meetings, I began to think I was in just another business meeting from the corporate world. Where was Jesus and His will in any of these discussions? It always seemed to be about what this person wanted to what that person wanted. I never ever heard anyone say, for example, "Let's prayerfully reflect on this and try to see what God's will in this matter is." If I wanted to see people behave badly and act childishly, I could do that at work and get paid a lot of money to sit through those meetings. I certainly didn't need to subject myself to it on my own time. To be clear, and it was made clear to me on several occasions, I was not an elected parish official. I was just a seminary student who was invited by Father, and I really didn't have a say in what they were voting on or arguing about.

After no more than two or three parish council meetings, I bailed out. I lost faith in that process faster than Peter walking across the water to meet Jesus. Not really knowing how to gracefully get out of these meetings, I simply found another church and another spiritual director where I could start over. I had found out what I did not want to do—diocesan pastoral work. It is necessary and a blessed vocation for those that are called to it; I felt clearly I was not.

With that experience behind me, my wife, Tami, and I (I had recently married Tami after we had been dating for several years) found a new church, and I found a new spiritual director. The new church was outside of the archdiocese of Detroit, so I would not be getting any financial support from the seminary, but it was the parish that I had raised my children in, and it was a large and active parish. The priest there was a family friend, and the large active parish gave both my wife and me opportunities to participate in different ministries; though, it was my wife who actually got involved. At that point, between work and seminary studies and the bad taste in my mouth from previous parish activities, I kept my distance and saved my ministry time for other activities.

Ministry—Hospice, Chaplaincy

I knew that I was called to serve from my time at the seminary and guidance from Sr. Mary and other significant spiritual figures in my life but was not really sure where to start. Living near Flint, Michigan, there were plenty of opportunities to serve others. I had previously done some service work in Flint, and it had usually been with my children. For many years, I was blessed to be able to donate platelets at an American Red Cross center near downtown Flint. I had really come to enjoy my few hours each couple of weeks donating. The ladies at the center were wonderful and very kind, and most importantly, I would get free cookies each time I donated. I am easily plied to do good works, just a few nice words and a few cookies, and I am ready to work until the sun goes down.

The experience of donating blood and platelets was enhanced for me when my children came along to donate as well. Seeing them donate not only their own blood but their own time to help others was really a proud moment as a parent. Donating platelets often takes several hours depending upon what your iron count is and if you are giving a single or a double donation. During this time, the donor sits pretty still in their chair and has a lot of time to watch TV, listen to the radio, or simply pray and contemplate. Often I would think about my giving of live-giving blood and platelets as an infinitesimally small example of Jesus sacrifice on the cross. Where Jesus sacrificed His body and blood until death for the savior of the entire human race, I was giving my life-giving blood and platelets to potentially save another person's life. I could see the chair or bed as an altar, and I was sacrificing my blood for the good of another. While minute in comparison to the sacrifice of so many others, it made the experience more than just a free cookie run and turned it into a holy experience for me.

Additionally, earlier in my life in Flint, I had taken my children and we had donated our time to work at the North End Soup Kitchen. This soup kitchen was always pretty busy and served the community in northeast Flint. This is the area where General Motors had once had a sprawling manufacturing complex, Buick City. A city within a city, the factory was closed and razed in the late twentieth century, and what was left behind was a huge vacant lot and many dilapidated houses. Where once scores of blue-collar workers lived and commuted the short distance to their jobs on the assembly line, now stood barely livable houses occupied by many who had no jobs and depended upon the soup kitchen to feed themselves and their children. I always felt it was a good experience for my children to see how fortunate they were to have what they had when so many other children their age and younger were walking across town just to get a good meal. The soup kitchen was run by Catholic Charities and never seemed to lack volunteers. Once while coaching high school wrestling, I set up a volunteer trip to the soup kitchen for the team. I had to book several months out as the kitchen was filled with groups looking to donate their time there. It was reassuring to see that there were so many willing to help.

As I looked at more ways to volunteer, I recalled my talks with Sr. Mary and how she felt I would be very good at hospice care. Though this did not seem to be something I was comfortable with, I thought that perhaps that is exactly why I should try it. So, searching online for Flint hospice volunteers, I was surprised to find several companies looking for volunteers to help out. I reached out to the one that seemed to be the best and had many good reviews. I received a callback within a day and was welcomed to come up and meet the volunteer coordinator. The meeting went well, and there were numerous forms I had to fill out, background checks, fingerprint verification, and hepatitis tests I had to get before I could start. There was training that was required; although, it was just a series of presentations put on by the coordinator for myself and a few other new volunteers. All totaled, it was about four to six weeks after we initially spoke that I was assigned my first patient.

When I was going through the hospice volunteer training, I was told I would be assigned patients in home settings as well as hospital and assisted-living facilities. Many of the patients I visited lived in houses that had been converted to assisted-living facilities. The hospice company had paid nurses, chaplains, and others on staff, and I was an unpaid volunteer. I was completely terrified for my first home visit on my own. I was assigned an older gentleman with Alzheimer and dementia. He lived in a large house with many other patients, and there were nurses on staff full time there. As I arrived at the house, I stopped and said a prayer to the Holy Spirit to show me what I needed to say or if I needed to say anything at all or just listen. I made this part of my routine whenever I met a new patient. As Jesus had told his apostles not to prepare speeches that the Holy Spirit would fill their mouths with the right words to speak, I leaned on that advice pretty heavily during my time in hospice.

    I was truly blessed to experience this ministry of hospice care. I knew going in that I would be establishing relationships that would be, due to the nature of the ministry, likely no more than six months long. I met so many amazing and wonderful people who were often so grateful just to have someone to talk to and share their story with. They often thanked me for taking my time to volunteer, but I felt I owed them a huge debt of gratitude for sharing their life stories with me and truly helping me to see Jesus in each person that I met. So often, what I came to see was that the people I was assigned to spend time with had little or no family connections to lean on. Through death or disagreements, they had no children or siblings that would come and see them. Many had achieved much in their careers, often at the expense of family. Many were alienated with their children, and even in their last months on earth, there was no reconciliation between family members. Many of the amazing people I visited had enough money to cover the cost of the round-the-clock care they were getting but had no one to share their final moments with. Others had strong families taking care of them, and the family members just needed a break. I would arrive, and the child or spouse would leave for a few hours to shop, take a walk, or otherwise recharge their hearts. They say you cannot give what you do not have, so these people were full of love and sharing it freely with their parents or spouses who were dying but needed a break to refill their hearts with love so they could continue to give it freely.

    It was a truly inspiring experience to spend these precious and holy moments with the people I visited. I always felt like I was the one being blessed during the visits and thanked God for giving me this opportunity. He never failed to provide me the words to share or the wisdom to just listen. A great example of this was when I met a new patient in Flint for the first time. An older gentleman, he had contracted cancer likely through his work and his love of smoking.

He quickly let me know when I walked in to meet him that he was a devout Baptist who knew his Bible and wondered why a young guy like me would want to volunteer "to spend time with old dying folks." When I told him, I attended the seminary and felt that this was what God had put on my heart to do, he was really ready to challenge me. A seminary? Was I Catholic? Did I read and know my Bible? He quizzed me on some of the less popular parts of the Old Testament. To his surprise, I was able to answer his questions, and he was surprised that a Catholic actually knew their Bible. What he did not know was that if he would have asked me these questions a year ago, I would not have been able to answer him. I had just completed several Old Testament courses at the seminary, so the questions he asked were familiar to me as I had just seen them on my final exams. It was not lost on me that God gives us what we need when we need it. I thanked God as I was leaving the house for preparing me, without me even knowing about, for these new people He was putting into my life. My patient and I became good friends, and his wife told me after he passed away that he looked forward to our visits each week. We had really cemented our friendship on one visit when his wife was gone, and he had asked me to drive into town really quick and pick him up a Coney dog with chili and onions. He missed having these, and his wife didn't like them, so she wouldn't get him any. I drove up to the Coney Island restaurant, they are on about every other corner in Flint and Detroit, and picked up a couple of Coney dogs and fries, and we shared them over a soda back at the house. This chili dog ministry was so appreciated by my patient.

People often tell me that they could never do hospice care as it would be too hard to make friends with someone only to see them die. I only experienced that issue a few times when my patient was young and clearly had many things they still wanted to do and children that were not ready for them to leave. I knew going in that the relationship we built would be short-term, and I was just there to be present for my patient and listen or laugh with them. Often, the patients were older and were ready to move on to the next step of their journey. There was sadness that there was pain they were going through, but with the palliative care they were provided, the pain was really minimized. Some of the most difficult times I had were when the patients did not have a belief in God, and they were scared of being alone and dying. I was not able to console or comfort them with faith-based discussions, and it was difficult for me. These examples too helped me to grow and, as St. Benedict writes in his prologue of the *Rule of St. Benedict*, bend the ear of my heart toward them. Instead of listening with the intent just to figure out what to say next, often missing the details and meaning of what someone was saying, I learned to listen deeply and let theirs words soak in and permeate my mind. There was no rush to provide a witty comeback or deep philosophical answer; just listen and learn and respond from the heart.

During my hospice care visits, I saw the vastly different ways in which the elderly in this country are cared for. On the positive side, there were the very nice extended care facilities, like small apartments, where the patients lived in their own room with nice windows and floral arrangements and nurses, with family members and staffs that attended to them. On the other end of the spectrum of my visits were the facilities, like old-age factories, that packed the patients in row by row. Often there would be three or four patients in a room that was barely big enough to fit the beds in. There would only be a few feet between beds, and it was all I could do to fit a chair in between to sit and talk to my patients. The nurses at some of these facilities seemed to be there clearly for financial reasons and treated the patients with a level of annoyance that seemed just below anger. I would walk down the hallways to get to my patient's room, and the people that were lined up in wheelchairs in the hallways would grab my arms and look vacantly up at me and ask me to please help them. I had to pray and ask for all the spiritual protection I could get before I would go into these facilities. There was such pain and anger and hostility just below the surface that it was tangible and heavy when I walked through the hallways. My heart broke for the patients I visited at these places. Often, these facilities were the low-cost options, and these patients had little or no savings and no family members to visit them. They spent all day in bed, sometimes barely conscious, and had a sadness that hung over them. I would try to engage them in sharing their life stories or, if they wanted to hear, share my stories about my children. These were often tough visits, but usually I would always see a ray of light from my patients at some point during the visit. It could sometimes see an ever so slight smile as we shared a story or a soft squeeze of my hand as I prepared to leave. The slightest sign that they appreciated the time together and for someone just to be present made these tough visits very worthwhile.

After doing hospice volunteer work for three or four years, my professional career moved my wife and I away from the Flint area, and I was forced to stop this ministry. To this day, I miss the relationships I built and the experiences I shared during these visits. I feel I was greatly enriched in one way or another by each patient I met with.

Having spent years in hospice care, I felt I was pretty well prepared when my studies at the seminary required that I complete my clinical pastoral education (CPE) credits by doing chaplain work at a local hospital. CPE is a requirement for many chaplain programs. During this time, chaplain interns like myself work with experienced chaplains to learn the process. I was blessed to be accepted to the CPE program at Beaumont Hospital in Royal Oak, Michigan. A beautiful hospital with a diverse staff and patient base, it was a great opportunity for me to learn. There were many other chaplain interns in the program, and they were much farther along in the process. As part of the program, each week all of us chaplains and interns would meet in the chaplain's office and sit in chairs in a large circle. In the program were chaplains of many different faiths. There were Mormons, Buddhists, Baptists, Methodists, and one other Catholic. It was quite the ecumenical meeting place. We would share our experiences for the week. We would share what meaningful events happened, and the other chaplains would very precisely reflect on our account of the story. It was meaningful and helpful to me to understand how people of other faiths saw the events differently from me. When I recounted a story of how blessed we were to have a shepherd like Jesus to lead us on our journey, the Buddhist chaplain quickly interceded. Was I calling us sheep? Because to him that was very demeaning. Sheep follow mindlessly, and being called a sheep seemed like an insult to him. For me, growing up Catholic, I always enjoyed the image of Jesus tending His flock, leading his sheep to the portico to allow us to enter eternal salvation. I quickly learned that what I saw as beautiful and comforting could be offensive to others. Lessons learned, know your audience.

After a month or so of shadowing other chaplains and more experienced interns, I was scheduled to work the night shift on my own. Coming in around 8:00 p.m., I would work until 5:00 a.m. on my own as most patients were sleeping and visits were minimal, often limited to emergencies and other specific events. To be able to contact us, we each carried pagers that let us know where to go, whom to call, and if we were needed immediately. Around 11:00 p.m., I got a page to come to the emergency department immediately. I figured that there had been an accident, and someone was asking for prayers or companionship while their loved one was in surgery. When I arrived, the nurse took me back into the staging area and directed me to an older lady who was there with her son. Her son was in the bed and with his hands and legs strapped down. I didn't see any visible signs of trauma, and no nurses or doctors were attending to him. I approached slowly, not sure what the emergency was. "Are you the chaplain?" the patient's mother asked as I walked up.

"Yes, I am. How can I help?" I asked a bit confused.

"Are you Catholic?" she asked.

"Yes, I am," I replied. An odd question to ask, I thought. Perhaps she wanted to say a rosary together. No problem, I carried a rosary in my pocket at all times for just such occasions. Her next question caused me to pause and think a bit before I answered.

"Do you believe in demonic possession and have you ever been part of an exorcism?" Well, how to answer that?

"Yes, I do believe it is possible for someone to become possessed, but no, I have never witnessed an exorcism except in a movie," I replied.

She then blurted out, "My son is possessed, and I need a Catholic priest to help." Well, there it was. Not really how I had planned to spend my first night solo as a chaplain. I hadn't really gotten to the part in the intern's manual about how to handle demonic possession. Very, very cautiously I moved forward with the discussion, grasping the rosary in my pocket very tightly, surprised I didn't break it.

"Well, I'm just a chaplain, and only an intern." I immediately added, "But can you tell me more?" She went on to tell me how her son was restrained because he had threatened to kill her and himself with a knife before the police arrived. An officer was stationed on the other side of the room, but since her son was restrained, the officer wasn't overly concerned about the situation.

She told me how her son had spoken to her in a different voice and spoke to her in Latin. Concerned because he had never studied Latin, so she was not sure how he was able to speak it fluently, she had previously contacted a local priest who was an exorcist. All the while she was telling me the story and the history of her son, I kept one eye on her and the other on her son just a few feet away in the bed. He was staring at me and had a strange smirk on his face. She asked me what she should do and could I help. I offered to contact the local priest and let him know of the situation. I also offered to say a prayer with her over her son. At that, her son started to make a strange sound and thrash about a bit. It seemed he, or whatever was inside him, was not overly anxious to be prayed over. I summoned what courage I could find and silently asked the Holy Spirit to guide me. I held his mother's hand and offered a short prayer for peace and comfort. I left the room after a few more minutes and took the priest's name she had talked to previously so I could call him later. When I shared the story in the roundtable discussion with the other chaplains, they said, to my surprise, "Oh, he's just mentally challenged. Don't worry about it."

I thought, *How does that explain his ability to speak fluently in Latin when he had never studied it?* I did share the experience with the local priest, and he told me he would contact the mother. I never heard further, but I figured if this was my first day of solo chaplaincy, I couldn't wait for what the future held in store for me.

My time as a chaplain intern was sadly cut short when I relocated for work. In the few months I studied and worked through the program, I saw that being a hospital chaplain was likely not what I wanted to continue to pursue. As strange as it sounds, the relationships I developed in hospice care were more meaningful than my visits as a chaplain in the hospital. In the hospital, I had a long list of people to visit, and I was not supposed to spend too much time with any one person. If they needed spiritual support, I was to provide that, but if not, just move along. I had to update the patient's files online with any notes from my visit, and since the records were reviewed by the insurance companies, it was very strict what I could and could not write. It seemed to be much more regimented and more of a job than a ministry to me. That's a bit unfair as good chaplains are indeed ministers, and perhaps if I get the chance to pursue this in another setting in the future, I will experience this more.

The one gift I did enjoy during my time in CPE training was the opportunity to pray with and over so many people. As a Catholic, charismatic prayer and praying over people was not something that the majority of the laity really did nor was comfortable with. Fortunately, remember God always provides, I had been involved in a charismatic prayer group at the seminary. The Fellowship of St. Paul was a voluntary group that met one Friday a month. There would be a guest speaker who would share their story, and then the large group would break into many smaller groups. The smaller groups would take turn laying hands on each other and praying over one another. This was unlike any other experience I had witnessed as a Catholic, and I asked several times if this was really an approved form of Catholic prayer. Assured by many professors that charismatic prayer harkened back to the very time of Jesus and the healing stories in the Gospel, I plunged forward. Usually when I am uncomfortable learning something, it means that it is something I need.

The experience of sitting in a chair in a small group in the middle of a room with everyone in your group standing over you and praying over you is indeed a powerful experience. I learned to give and accept prayer. At first, I felt so strange saying prayers over someone. I felt like I had to think of some prayerful and powerful thing to say. Instead, when I learned to just be quiet in my mind and get out of the way, the words would just come. I was often surprised by what I said when praying over someone. *Wow, that was really beautiful and meaningful,* I thought. *I wonder where that came from.*

CHAPTER 10
Mystical Experiences

Do you not think that there are things which you cannot understand, and yet which are; that some people see things that others cannot? But there are things old and new which must not be contemplated by men's eyes, because they know—or think they know—some things which other men have told them. Ah, it is the fault of our science that it wants to explain all; and if it explains not, then it says there is nothing to explain.

—Bram Stoker

The Devil Is in the Details and My Hallway

Imagine driving down an old country road with the windows down and the wind whistling by you. As you slow down and stop on the side of the road to look off into the distance at the rising mountains, all is quiet and peaceful. After a few minutes, you get back into your car and just appreciate the beauty that is around you. You turn on the radio to see if there is any music to accompany you on your journey, and being so far removed from everywhere, nothing but static. You leave the radio on and continue on your journey. Every now and then, a station will come in, and the faint sounds of an old familiar tune can be heard and then fade away as you continue on. As you drive further, the same station that played that old familiar tune is overpowered by an obnoxious station that blares commercials and music that you can't stand to listen to. I liken this experience to what happened to me spiritually when I went through my divorce and then started to attend the seminary.

I had been driving down the road of life with the radio off, not listening for God's voice and just enjoying the view of what was immediately in front of me. When I started attending the seminary, I turned my spiritual radio on. Every now and then, I would pick up a good channel and be encouraged by what I heard. Then, as I was still navigating a particularly treacherous path of life, due to my own making, I would pick up a signal that was completely upsetting and would shock me enough to try to turn down the radio. I had a choice, either shut the radio off or try to get to a better part of the neighborhood to improve my life and start picking up better signals.

In the apartment in which I lived immediately after I was divorced, the radio was flooded with lots of bad wavelengths. It was so loud and tangible that when people would visit, they would tell me of being freaked out and picking up a bad vibe. It got to the point that my sons didn't really enjoy coming over because they could feel something was not right in the apartment.

Not surprisingly, after my divorce in 2010, my lifestyle choices and desire to seek self-satisfaction through partying and drinking had opened up my spiritual antennae to all sorts of bad stations. Perhaps the most disturbing for me occurred one night when I was alone in the apartment. Like most nights, I had gone to bed by myself as my girlfriend Judy had her own house with her kids and did not spend the night very often at my house. That night, I had gone to bed fairly early knowing that I would have to get up early the next day to drive to work and wanted to get some rest. I have never been a great sleeper, and this night was no exception. Tossing and turning, I could not believe how hot it was in the apartment. I assumed the air conditioner had broken because I was sweating due to the heat. I remember quite vividly waking up to toss off my covers. As I looked at the end of my bed and in the doorway of my bedroom, I saw someone standing there as clear as day. I was startled and didn't know what to say. Startled both because there was someone, or more accurately something, standing in my room. The person standing in my doorway was not Judy or either of my sons, but instead it was something I could not identify. I recall it had legs and arms and looked human, but its head was some beastly looking thing with curly horns. It didn't say anything to me but just sort of stood there and laughed in a low guttural kind of way. I was scared out of my mind. So, after lifting weights and working out for years and being a pretty big and strong guy, I did what seemed natural, I pulled the blankets over my head and yelled to this thing to get out and prayed to Jesus and Mary to save me. I figured, shit, I better look to see if this thing is coming closer or what the hell was happening, so I pulled the sheets down enough to see and whomever or whatever was standing there had left.

I laid there wondering what in the hell I had just seen and what had happened. I had to go to the bathroom, but there was no way I was getting out of bed at that point, and I laid there and reached over to turn on a night-light. After I had calmed down for a few minutes, I got the nerve to get out of bed and walk over to the bathroom that was connected to the bedroom. I looked around the apartment turning on every light as I entered each room. It was a small apartment, so it didn't take long. Completely shook up, I got up and used the bathroom, got some water, and tried to lay back down to sleep. I found it impossible to close my eyes for more than a few minutes without sneaking a look over to the door to make sure I was alone.

I have reflected on this experience over the years and am sure I had not just seen a shadow or reflection. There was a small night-light in the hallway just beyond my room that provided adequate light to clearly illuminate the area. What I saw, I saw as clearly as someone standing not more than ten feet away from you. The low laughing sound was harsh and cruel and struck deep within me. It is an experience that I will remember as long as I live. I had left my spiritual radio on and had picked up a very bad signal that was being broadcast at full volume. As I shared my experience of this with Judy and my sons, the boys were not too surprised and immediately said they felt something wrong with the place. I have no doubt it was not the apartment itself that was bad but the energy and spirits I brought into it with my choices and actions that caused this thing to manifest itself so clearly.

Healing Seminar—Gift of Prophecy

Shortly after this event while numerous unexplainable things seemed to be happening to me and around me, I had the opportunity to attend a three-day seminar at the seminary on the different charisms of the Holy Spirit. Put on by the seminary, they had brought in an individual from England that had done some pretty miraculous and documented healings throughout the world. Judy and I attended, not really knowing what to expect in the days ahead.

The seminar started pretty mundanely on a Friday night when we all gathered and asked for prayers and the Holy Spirit's intercession over the weekend to help us draw closer to the Lord and receive whatever gifts He had in store for us.

Returning Saturday morning, we were ready to really dig into this experience and see what would come from it. The first thing we did was a general healing and exorcism of all those in the room. The speaker called upon the Holy Spirit and prayed for us and asked that any unclean spirits be removed from us and for us to be open to the gifts of the spirit. Within no more than twenty seconds after this, a middle-aged housewife behind me whom I had had coffee and sweet rolls with no more than thirty minutes prior began growling, making strange noises, and almost convulsing in her chair. The people at the seminary who were facilitating this had been advised that at this time in the seminar, something like this might happen, so there were several folks ready to help the lady. They all gathered around her and kind of shielded what was going with her from the rest of the group and asked that we remain focused on the prayer that was being offered on stage. I thought, *How can I not focus on what was going on behind me!* I tried my best not to be distracted or pay attention to the seemingly demonic spirit that was being exercised no more than twenty feet from me. Eventually, through prayer and laying on of hands, they were able to calm the lady and quietly escort her out of the room. *Wow*, I thought, *this was going to be some weekend after all!*

One of the significant events of that weekend occurred later that afternoon as we broke into two-man groups for an exercise on the gift of prophecy. You were required to pick someone you had never met and knew nothing about. Not really knowing what to expect, I partnered up with a gentleman that was sitting a few rows behind me. The leader of the exercise asked that we turn our chairs so that we were facing our partners and move them close so we were almost knee to knee so we could grasp each other's hands. Then the leader told us that we were to close our eyes and concentrate on a message from God that He might be sending us to share with our partner. Be open and docile to the workings of the Holy Spirit, and share some personal message for your partner. While this sounds easy enough, it was incredibly intimidating. I was going to tell my partner some message that the Holy Spirit had supposedly given me about him. I had no idea if the guy was married or not, if he had children or not. I knew nothing about this guy, so how was this going to work? Slowly, I closed my eyes and asked for the Holy Spirit to fill my heart and give me some meaningful message to share with my partner. Slowly, after what seemed like an eternity but was likely no more than a few minutes, a little picture came into my head of my partner in his backyard planting flowers with a young girl that he seemed to really love. There was a rock garden surrounding the area, and he was on his knees planting, and she was handing him dirt and flowers.

Well, what did all this mean? I didn't know if he even had kids, and perhaps someone had died, and I was going to hurt his feelings. Okay, trust in the Lord, I told myself as I sheepishly shared with him the details of what I had seen. Slowly he listened, and after a few moments, a tear came to his eye. Oh no, what had I done now, I wondered. As I finished my story, he tightened his grip on my hands and thanked me. He told me that the young girl I had seen was his daughter, and she had just gone off to college, and he was missing her desperately. When she was young, they used to work together in his backyard and plant flowers. This message I shared with him gave him great comfort and brought back loving and happy memories of the time with his daughter. I was stunned. How had the Holy Spirit given me a message that truly meant something to this man whom I had just met. I was truly amazed, and from that moment on, I truly began to believe in the power of prophecy. This gift of prophecy is not through any innate gift that we have or special power or technique, just simply as a gift from the Holy Spirit for those that ask for it in earnest. I felt blessed to have been touched by the Spirit for even just a brief moment.

Speaking in Tongues

As part of the Fellowship of St. Paul meetings on Friday nights at the seminary, we were often asked to pray over people and to be open to the gifts of the Spirit. Once a year, the seminary hosts a weekend event for the Fellowship of St. Paul where we dig deeper into charismatic prayer and really seek to immerse ourselves in the tongues of fire that scripture speaks of. There is a charismatic prayer service in the chapel, and the event it usually well attended with people who are very active in their faith. It was during this weekend retreat that I learned of the practice of speaking in tongues. Speaking in tongues is mentioned often in scripture. For example, in the Acts of the Apostles, it reads, "When Paul placed his hands on them, the Holy Spirit came on them, and they spoke in tongues and prophesied" (Acts 19:6). Still, like much of scripture, I was not familiar with these examples at that time, and the whole idea of asking for the Holy Spirit to come down and give me the gift of speaking in tongues seemed strange and definitely outside the boundaries of what I thought Catholicism found acceptable. Again, I was reassured that it was acceptable to ask for this gift and that it was just simply another way to pray.

So, reluctantly I agreed and allowed myself to be prayed over by one of the professors who was leading the retreat. He prayed over me in a language I clearly understood, English, and then slipped into sounds I was not familiar with. He finished by saying I should try this and see if anything came to me by opening myself up to the spirit. At first, I was a little embarrassed to ask to speak in strange sounds or languages. But slowly, and very quietly, I started to speak in some language I was not familiar with. I thought to myself that really, I was just making sounds and that I was not really speaking in tongues. The noises come out of me couldn't possibly be a language though it did sound a bit Middle Eastern, which made sense as I had spent a good bit of time in Egypt.

As I became more and more comfortable with this, perhaps less intimidated because most everyone else was speaking some language or sounds that I could not discern, I just gave myself into it, and it felt like opening up the spigot on a hose. When I prayed in English, even when allowing the Spirit to talk through me, I had to form my words and put sentences together. When speaking in tongues, there was no filter, no need to form words I knew and no intelligible sentences to construct. I simply let the sounds flow through me like water through a hose. I just went on and on. I closed my eyes, thought of God in the light of salvation, and just let whatever sounds wanted to come out to come out. It was like I had cut through a filter and tapped into a main line, like I was a branch that was directly connected to the vine, and the living energy was coming through me. It was a pretty cool experience, and I started to pray this way more often. Often I would do it in private or when reading scripture at home by myself. It was not a prayer form that I would use when attending Sunday mass at the local parish for fear they would call the priest or police for help. It certainly sounded strange, and I often wondered if it was an actual language I was speaking or just sounds that formed in my mind. Regardless and likely more importantly, it was a new and exciting way for me to tap into the love and energy that God has for each of us. I came to use this gift as just another tool to deepen my prayer and my connection to our Father in heaven. To be sure, one has to trust in God in this process and overcome the fear of sounding dumb or not doing it right. Just trust in the Lord and be open to His urgings. Some people very much enjoy this type of prayer while it is just not for others. For me, I found it freeing and a way to really open myself up to whatever messages God had for me.

Ghosts in the Machine and My Dreams

In 2013, after my third year of studies at the seminary, I had married Tami, my current wife, a wonderful woman who was very spiritual and supported my studies and challenged me daily on what

I had learned. We had started an amazing spiritual journey together, and I dove even deeper into my faith. For whatever reason, after we got married, the *radio* seemed to be turned up to full blast, and I was picking up spiritual wavelengths throughout the day and most especially at night.

I had always been aware and able to perceive whatever you are comfortable calling the, spirits, ghosts, whatever. They were present in different forms, but I was so involved in my own thoughts and desires that I often kept the volume down very low and was able to filter these experiences down, so they were almost imperceptible. As I grew in faith and opened myself up to a true covenantal and sacramental bond of love with my wife, the filters came off, and the voices and spirits came in full blast.

There was never a night that I was able to sleep without seeing and hearing hundreds of spirits. I would no sooner fall asleep that I would be engaged in conversations with someone about something. I would be talking out loud, and my wife would wake me, and I would be completely disoriented as to where I was and whom I was speaking to. I was so deeply engaged in listening to the people that came to me, and they were so vivid that when I woke up, I could sometimes not distinguish what was "real." At first, it was very interesting as usually the people were kind and wanted to share some information with me. Often they would ask for help, and I usually would have no idea how to provide what they were asking for.

As the nights went on, it became more and more of an issue. I would go to bed only to see twenty to thirty people lined up by my bed waiting to speak with me. It was a little chaotic as everyone wanted to speak at once, and I could not sleep. It was not so much voices I would hear in my head; it was full on conversations, extremely vivid images, and a lot of energy. It was starting to be a problem as I would often spend hours each night engaged in these discussions and would wake up completely drained the next morning.

At times, the visitors were not so friendly and were incredibly dark and, well, scary. They would seek to grab me and pull me off the bed. My wife would have to wake me up as I was thrashing about trying to fight back against these unfriendlies. When these folks came to visit me, the others who usually spoke to me made a hasty exit, as if they wanted nothing to do with these visitors.

Finally, I felt like I needed to do something for my own sake so I could get some rest and not be struggling each night. I was a little hesitant because often there were incredible experiences during these visits where I would be traveling to beautiful places and see incredibly bright lights. I recall being asleep and seeing such a bright light that it hurt my eyes and woke me up. I could quickly close my eyes and go right back to where I had been before waking up. While this ability to return to where I had been was good on these amazing journeys, it was not so good when these dark visitors were waiting for me just on the other side of consciousness.

My wife and I had been attending group meditation sessions at a yoga studio in Flushing, Michigan, around this time. The owner of the study was very good at leading and directing the meditation sessions and was also very gifted spiritually. After one particular session where she had sensed some issues with me, she asked if everything was going well or if there was anything going on. I told her about my issues with the visitors I had each night and how it was affecting my ability to sleep. She graciously offered to help. So, after everyone had left but my wife and I, she sat with us in the front room. After describing what the issues were in detail, she offered some prayers for me and advised me on some prayers I might say. She also blessed a beautiful bracelet of beads and asked that I wear them to bed each night. Going home, satisfied that we had tried to address the issue, we were hopeful I would be able to get a little sleep. Thankfully the prayers and the bracelet were helpful, and I was able to once again quiet the crowd that sought my attention and finally get some rest.

As work picked up and I was transferred to a new job that was exponentially busier than the one I had already had, I quickly shifted my focus to my work, and by the time I hit the pillow each night, I was mentally and physically exhausted and fell quickly to sleep. There were no issues with dreams or sleep after that.

Fast-forward four years down the road from my prayer sessions at the yoga studio. I had been blessed with amazing opportunities and had retired from work and was now living and volunteering at a

Benedictine monastery in Atchison, Kansas. We had sold our homes and given away the bulk of our belongings and had spent the previous year traveling the country. Free from the demands of a daily job, I was able to focus on prayer and scripture and opened myself more deeply to the urgings of the spirit. It was within this new framework of my life that my friends, the visitors, came knocking again at the door inside my head.

At the monastery where we were living and volunteering, the sisters had provided us with a beautiful old home to live in. The house, called Marywood Hall, was built in the nineteenth century and had all the historic charm of a well maintained one-hundred-plus-year-old home. The wood working was exquisite, the windows were large and numerous, and it was a wonderful place to call home while we volunteered with the community. Throughout the years, many of the sisters in the community had called this house home for some period of their time here. The sisters came to Atchison in the 1860s, and there was a dynamic history of amazing women who lived and prayed here. The sisters are deeply spiritual, and the walls and woodwork in Marywood are covered in memories and practically drip with prayers, both those answered and unanswered. Through over a hundred years of prayerful lamentations to God in this house, the very fiber and structure of the house is embedded with spiritual energy.

With me living and praying with the sisters daily, I had fully opened myself up to God in prayer and contemplation. I had let down any walls that had been protected to keep unwanted visitors out. This proved to be a mistake on my part, as I found out quickly after I moved into Marywood.

Seeking to deepen my prayer life even further, I had started to pray night prayer. Typically, I would get up around 1:00 a.m. or 2:00 a.m. to use the restroom, and after finishing, instead of returning to our room to go back to sleep, I would go to a smaller bedroom adjacent to ours and say my evening prayers from the Divine Office. Usually taking no more than fifteen minutes, I would then try to go back to bed in that small room, so as not to disturb my wife, fully spiritually charged after my session of prayers.

One night, after tossing and turning a bit after prayers before finally falling back to sleep, I was bolted awake by the sound of a young girl screaming in our house. As it was just my wife and I and one other volunteer living here, I knew the scream had not come from any of us, but the scream had been clear as knife cutting through the blackness of the night. *Damn*, I thought, *not this again.* I sat up and waited again for any other noises of commotions. Nothing. I must have imagined it, I thought as I hesitantly put my head back down, one eye cracked open staring at the open door at the end of the bed. Being very tired, I eventually drifted back to sleep. Very quickly I was joined in my slumber by someone that I can only call a demon or Satan or whatever is dark and evil. He looked at me face-to-face; he seemed like he was only a few feet from my face and pointed his finger outward and across a room I had never seen before. I saw a mother murdering her daughter. A voice cried that she, the daughter, was only five years old, and I could see the girl was terrified. The evil one's face morphed into that of the girl's mother, and it seemed to me as if the mother had been possessed by this evil one, and this is what led her to kill her daughter. I heard someone say that the girl had been poisoned, but I couldn't understand why the little girl was screaming. After the girl had quieted, the mother turned at me, and her face was twisted to look like something between her face and the face of rage, the face of darkness and fear. It was a hideous site. The creature growled out to me as he pointed his finger in my face. "You could have prevented this." With that, I awoke with a start and hopped out of bed. I walked back into my bedroom where my wife was sound asleep and cuddled up tightly next to her. "Hey, say a prayer for me and put a shield of protection around me. I need some help," I asked her as she listened, half awake and half asleep.

"Sure," she said as she pushed me away to give herself some room to turn over. I finally fell asleep only to hit my snooze button on my alarm an hour or so later.

I was so rattled by the dream; I was still thinking about it when I woke up. I could remember all the details very vividly. I thought, *What the heck. Let's Google some of the details and see if anything like this happened.* I would like to say, to my surprise, but it really wasn't, what I had dreamed about had happened just a few weeks earlier no more than twenty minutes where I had grown up. A mother had killed her five-year-old daughter, and the theory the police were working with was that she had given her prescription pills and poisoned her before killing herself as well. Apparently there had been a history of abuse, so I thought perhaps that abuse was the screams I had heard. Reflecting further, it made sense about the voice I had heard about her being poisoned. As I dug deeper, I saw a picture of the mother, and she looked very much like the woman I had seen in my dream the night before. I did not see a picture of the house where the tragedy had occurred, but I could describe from my dream what it looked like, and I wondered if it would match up. I thought hard about what the message meant that I could have done something about this. Perhaps it was because I had stifled my "gift" years ago and was not listening when someone, perhaps this little girl, had called out for help. Perhaps it was just a trick of the evil one who seeks to discourage us and turn us away from God. I shared this with my wife, and ever wise, she suggested what I could do now to help them both was to pray for them. Having seen their names from the new article I had just Googled, I kept them both in prayer for many days.

This episode reminded me that no matter where I am at and whatever the situation, a beautiful old house at a monastery or traveling on the road, while it is my calling to be open to the gifts and urgings of the Holy Spirit, I have to be careful and not let just any frequency that is out there blast across my spiritual radio.

Silent Retreats at Manresa

I can't recall how I first heard of Manresa Jesuit retreat center in Michigan. Perhaps it was because all the seminarians had to spend some time there for a directed silent retreat in Ignatian spirituality.

JOURNEY INTO LOVE

St. Ignatius was the founder of the Jesuit order and has developed a unique spirituality that focuses on Christ through silent prayer and reflection and examination of one's conscience. It is a beautiful spirituality that I am only vaguely familiar with, but one that attracted me nonetheless to this beautiful retreat center. In the middle of a moderately busy suburban area, it is like an oasis of peace in the midst of the city hustle. When you enter the grounds off of the busy street, you immediately drive in behind a forest of mature trees and beautifully landscaped grounds, and within thirty seconds of waiting in traffic and inhaling exhaust fumes, you are transported to a quiet habitat of peace.

Before I did my first retreat at Manresa, I drove the small roads that led to the guesthouse and pulled over and parked my car. I got out and walked slowly around the grounds. Looking at the statues, the trees, the sculptures, and quiet sitting places, I was amazed at the beauty. Looking to the east at the row of trees that separates Manresa from the reality of the adjacent road, I noticed a large cave-like area. It had to have been man made, but it looked like a cave of stones from a Middle Eastern country. As I approached, I saw it to be a grotto with the Blessed Mother inside. Hundreds of rosaries were laid across the stones and the lights and the statues. All the rosaries had been left by faithful souls asking for their prayers to be lifted up through Mary's intervention to her son Jesus. It was a powerful first image on Manresa.

For my first retreat, I figured I would really give it my all. Instead of joining with a larger group and being directed, I was going to do an individual self-directed retreat. Instead of only going for a few days, checking in on Friday and leaving Sunday, I was going to stay all week. I was going to fast, pray in silence, and talk to God in the quiet of the retreat center. I would leave my phone out in the car so as not to be tempted by it, and I was going to pray by myself to have a closer connection to God. Manresa, like most Jesuit retreat centers, facilitates this by providing a holy meeting place with a complete emphasis on silence. No phones are allowed. Talking among guests and one another or the priests is not recommended outside of offices and chapel. The idea is to be quiet and listen to God.

After meeting with one of the Jesuit priests who lived in residence there, I shared with him my plan. He asked if I had ever done a silent retreat before. I told him I had not, this was the first. He suggested that while fasting does have its place in spirituality, he recommended that I don't do it on my first retreat. His concern was that I would spend the week thinking about how hungry I was and lose focus on why I came there in the first place. I would not be able to hear God over the grumbling in my stomach. I agreed and was glad I did as the food that the kitchen staff provided was excellent.

Inside of Manresa, on the second floor, is a small prayer room that is called the cave. It is an ordinary square room, perhaps twelve feet by twelve feet. What is unique is that it is completely quiet in there, and the lights can be dimmed to whatever level you want. There is both a chair and a kneeler in the cave. On the wall farthest from where you enter and in front of the kneeler is a crucifix with a candle next to it. On the wall to your right as you enter is a small padded bench where you can sit or even lay and pray. Above that bench is a sculpture that immediately grabbed my attention and radiates like a bright light in my mind even to this day. No more that twelve or fourteen inches, the sculpture is of the head of a young Mary. The sculpture came out of a square base, but what makes it unique is the orientation. It appears that Mary would be in the next room and sticking her head through the wall to see what you are doing, straining to hear your voice and your prayers. It is so realistic; it appears that Mary is in the room with you. Often when praying my rosary in the cave, I would wait quietly, sure that Mary was going to turn her head toward me and offer some sage advice. Though that never happened, it was a powerful experience.

Throughout the first week, I had many times where I was overcome to write both poetry and prose. The words I wrote seemed to not come from me, but instead, I was just a conduit from which they flowed through me and onto the page. Reading them later, they seemed foreign to me. Like I had not thought of these and was only the scribe to capture these thoughts. I also spent a lot of time reading scripture and reflecting. I would meet once a day with one of the priests, and he would ask me how it was going, if I had any questions or concerns. Typically, he would then give me a short reading assignment like, "I feel as if you should read Luke 4 chapter 6 to 14 tonight." I would then read it and reflect on what message I got from it.

As I was really enjoying reading, I decided to just open up the Bible and read from a book I was not too familiar with. I open up and looked at the table of contents and pointed immediately to the book of Sirach. Interesting, I thought. I knew from scripture study at the seminary that Sirach is included in Catholic Bibles but not in the Protestant Bible. Well, what is God trying to tell me here, I thought. I read Sirach and found many interesting and thought-provoking stories. After reading for some time, I put the Bible down and thought, *That's enough for now. I should go for a walk around the retreat center and reflect on what I had just read. Why did I pick this book out, and was this what I was supposed to be reading?* I left my room and shut my door without locking it; there is a level of trust you have when staying in a retreat house. As I walked around the large house, I came across a small private chapel. This little chapel could hold no more than four or five people and was used for very small ceremonies or masses. Later that week, I would have a private mass with one of the priests in this small chapel. As I sat down in the chapel to look around, I noticed a small old Bible on the table next to the window. As I walked over and looked, I was shocked. The Bible in this small chapel was on the exact chapter and verse of Sirach as I had left off in my room. I instantly felt that I was being directed that yes, indeed, this is what I should be reading. The Bible has hundreds of pages, and for this Bible in this chapel to be left open to the exact location I had left off when I stopped reading in my room was beyond coincidence.

Experiences after Receiving Eucharist

There are few places I feel closer to God than when I am in nature. To sit next to a river as it winds its way through a secluded section of the forest or to sit atop a mountain and look down across all of visible creation makes me feel as if I am seeing nature as God intended and brings me so close to Him.

When in nature, I feel as if I am close to God. When I receive the Eucharist, I have the palpable feeling that Jesus Christ, who died on the cross for me, is now physically a part of me through my receiving Him. It is an intimate and powerful experience. As a Catholic, we believe that the bread we eat on Sunday and the wine we drink is actually the real presence of Jesus Christ. This bread and wine are in fact transformed into the essence of his actual body and blood. Though the physical properties of the bread and wine remain, it is transformed in essence to the body and blood of Christ. Thus, I can never feel closer to Jesus than when I receive His body and blood. He becomes part of me, and we share in this physical body. It is because of this experience of actually sharing my body with Jesus that I feel intimately connected to Him at this time.

Often after receiving the Eucharist, I will go into a very deep place of prayer. Usually I can experience a quietness, and I reflect on the sound of the voices of those who are singing carrying our prayers up to God. I also can see the heavens opening up and a brilliant light shining down upon me. I am often taken back to medieval times when I hear the people slowly shuffling by and think this exact process of receiving the body and blood goes back over thousands of years. The language has changed, and different songs are played, but people gathering on Sunday, experiencing the transubstantiation, when the bread and wine is transformed, and intimately connecting with Jesus has happened billions of times. It is estimated that there are 1.2 billion Catholics in the world. Of that number, less than half receive the Eucharist on a regular basis, but often do once or twice a year. Imagine that number and all the Catholics throughout the ages and this process within the church has literally taken place billions of times. And yet, each time I receive the Eucharist, it is a new and humbling experience. Jesus is real and relevant to me each day and each time we share our body and blood; it is a new experience.

These are powerful moments or prayer and reflection for me. I am humbled so much when the priest or eucharistic minister places the body of Christ in my hand so that I may place it in my mouth. I am hesitant to even touch what I believe to be the body of Christ, of God himself, the creator of the *universe*. Think about the overwhelming grace of that. The creator of the universe, who has existed before time, loves me enough to come to me where I am in church and allow Himself to be shared with me each day. It is beyond humbling if I truly stop and think about the magnitude of what I am allowed to experience each day.

There are special times when I have quieted my mind and allowed myself not to be distracted by whatever may be going on in church at that time, where I have experienced special gifts from the Father. One of these experiences was so powerful I recall it to this day. I had entered church in a particularly reverent and prayerful state. I had listened closely to the readings from the Gospel, and they all really resonated with me. As the priest blessed the bread and wine, I closed my eyes and could see Jesus around the table with his apostles and likely his friend Mary Magdalen and perhaps His mother as well. As I walked up to the altar to receive the Eucharist, I was overwhelmed with a sense of gratitude for sharing in the life of the almighty. It was when I returned to the pew for prayer and reflection that I was overwhelmed with a beautiful vision. Though I was still kneeling in the pew, I had left the church. I was with Jesus on Golgotha, the hill where He was crucified. Instead of looking up at Him hanging on the cross, He allowed me to come and experience what He saw as He looked down. I was behind his right shoulder and could feel the warm wind blowing across His body as he hung there in agony, nails through his hands and feet. Instead of despair, He was looking forward across the hills and the homes in the distance. As He looked ahead, a circle appeared in front of Him, and He was seeing throughout time at all the people who would offer up their thanksgiving for His sacrifice for them. I think this was a gift from His Father to show Jesus the magnitude of the gift He was giving all mankind. I was deeply moved that Jesus had allowed me to enter into this moment and share this gift with Him. I had never seen the moment of crucifixion from this perspective. Looking down, I saw a few of Jesus's loved ones gathered below and sobbing, various townspeople and soldiers around. It was a moving experience to somewhat see this moment through the eyes of Jesus Himself. It seemed as if this experience lasted for quite some time, but I knew it was only a few minutes as the remainder of the parishioners in the pews went forward and received the Eucharist. I did not want to leave, but slowly, I came down from Jesus's side, and the image went off into the light, and I was cognizant of where I was and what was happening around me. It seems whenever I have that deep connection, I want to remain with Jesus or Mary, and it is they who dictate when it is my time to come back. I feel deeply grateful for each of these experiences I have had as they are gifts to further sustain me on my journey here on this earth.

CHAPTER 11
A More Mature Faith

A man knows when he has found his vocation when he stops thinking about how to live and begins to live.
—Thomas Merton

Spiritual Direction

Saint Ignatius of Loyola was born in Spain at the end of the fifteenth century and died in 1556. A soldier who had fought in wars, he was confined to a hospital bed when his leg was hit by a cannonball. During this time, since there were limited books available to read, he took up reading about the lives of saints and in particular, Jesus Christ. St. Ignatius became deeply interested in Christ, and his heart was set on fire with the love of God. Over the course of his life, Ignatius's newfound passion for Christ would give spiritual birth to the Society of Jesus, or as they are more commonly referred to today, the Jesuits.

One of the most notable Jesuits in the early twenty-first century in the United States is Fr. James Martin, SJ. Fr. Martin has openly shared his thoughts and beliefs in the equality of all people and the love that Jesus has for the least of us. In addition, Fr. Martin has taken a very public and vocal stance that the members of the LGBT community are deeply loved by Jesus as are all people. At this time in the history of our culture, there is great debate about gender identification and sexual orientation, and Fr. Martin has taken a position and written and shared his beliefs and understanding of the teachings of Jesus. Fr. Martin's perspective has upset many "conservative" Catholics who also have strong feelings, often contrary to Fr. Martin's, on these matters.

Fr. Martin is an accomplished author, and one of his books, *Jesus: A Pilgrimage*, has an excellent quote on spiritual direction. In it, he writes,

> Spiritual direction helps people notice where God is active in their lives. While it may overlap with a number of other practices, spiritual direction is neither psychotherapy (which focuses mainly on the psychological underpinnings of a person's problem), nor pastoral counseling (which focuses mostly on problem solving in a spiritual setting, nor confession (which focuses on sin and forgiveness).

With this understanding of the intent of spiritual direction, I can see the role that my spiritual director, Fr. Leo Cachat, has had in helping me notice where God is active in my life. Without this direction, I am certain I would have missed many of the blessed experiences I have had in prayer.

Because of the unfavorable experiences I had in parish council at the church I had grown up in, I had left that parish and the spiritual director I had there. As having a spiritual director was required for the academic program I was in at the seminary, I was not sure where to turn and prayed for direction regarding this matter. I decided I would attend a self-directed retreat at Manresa Jesuit retreat house in Michigan. I felt that time alone in prayer would be helpful to discern who would be the best fit for this important role in my spiritual life.

As part of the retreat practice at Manresa, even if you are doing a self-directed retreat, they assign a priest, all of the priests there are Jesuits, to meet with you once a day to review how things are going, to listen to your observations and perhaps suggest readings or share their thoughts. I was blessed to be assigned Fr. Leo as my guide that week. As I walked into his office the first time, I was struck by the diversity of religious items I saw. Looking around, I saw traditional pictures of Jesus and Mary but also many Eastern types of imagery and quotes from different religious traditions. As I got to know Fr. Leo, I found that he had lived for several decades in Nepal and studied with many of the authors that I was currently reading. Having studied with Fr. Bede Griffiths and Anthony DeMello, I was able to ask him firsthand about the books from these gentlemen that I was reading. I felt an instant connection with Fr. Leo and a shared spiritual curiosity.

At the conclusion of the week as the retreat was ending, I asked Fr. Leo if he had time to take on another spiritual directee and if he would be my spiritual director. Without hesitation, he said yes and let me know the boundaries of our relationship as director and directee. To maintain a clear role, it was his practice that director and directee not really associate outside of the sessions. This was acceptable to me, and I was excited to have such a gifted and wise soul as Fr. Leo to help me on my journey and to help me notice where God was active in my life and what things I was holding onto that were blocking my relationship with God.

The spiritual direction meetings usually lasted about an hour or so. I would share openly with Fr. Leo about my prayer life and what things were going well, what I was struggling with, and what issues still troubled me as it related to my faith life. Fr. Leo listened and would often say something that was right on point. There were a lot of "aha, why didn't I think of that" sort of moments.

I suspect that through our meetings he sensed that there was a missing component of my faith. Due to the issues I had with my fathers when I was young, I think my prayer life was very maternally based and heavily reliant on Holy Mother Mary and perhaps unbalanced. In one session, perhaps because of this reason, Fr. Leo shared a prayer card with me that was written by two Detroit priests. This card was the Hail Joseph prayer. It recognizes Joseph for the fatherly role he played in Jesus's life and perhaps because of my own lack of a father figure spoke to me very directly.

The St. Joseph Prayer is as follows—

> Hail Joseph, full of the family of God
> The Lord is in your arms
> Blessed are thou among men
> And blessed is thou Son Jesus
> Holy Joseph, foster father of Jesus and husband of Mary
> Pray for us now
> And especially at the hour of our death

This prayer really seemed to resonate with me. So much in fact that I started to incorporate it into my rosary. To be clear, how I pray my rosary is of my own making and not likely to be endorsed by traditional Catholics, but for me, it helped me deepen my prayer life. Traditionally, when saying the rosary, you recite the "Our Father" prayer on each of the large prayer beads, then recite the "Hail Mary" prayer on each of the ten small beads. You then recite the "Glory Be" and the "Oh My Jesus" prayer before starting the entire cycle again on the large prayer bead. There are other prayers as well, but this is the general crux of the rosary. This cycle is done five times before you are complete. The "Our Father" and "Hail Mary" prayers are basically taken directly from scripture, so in the end, you spend about thirty minutes reciting scripture and reflecting on how the verses speak to you that day.

I will often alternate between the "Hail Mary" and the "Hail Joseph" prayer when praying the smaller beads. I have found that this really gives me a sense of the entire Holy Family, and perhaps coming from a somewhat fractured family as a child, this sense of completeness speaks to me and draws me deeper into prayer. I have my spiritual director, Fr. Leo, to thank for this development in my prayer life.

I can recall many long walks around the property at the Manresa retreat center where Fr. Leo lives and provides spiritual direction. During these walks outside, I would recite my modified rosary and feel an overwhelming sense of peace and happiness. I would pray that Joseph intercede for me and show me how to be a good father and husband. Jesus was many things while on earth, but he was not a father nor was he a husband. I look to Joseph as my role model for both of these important roles of my life. It is also believed by many Catholics that praying for St. Joseph's intercession will also result in a peaceful death when our journey here on earth is complete, so that's not too bad a benefit either.

Though the spiritual direction was a requirement of the seminary for the course of study I was taking, I have found it invaluable in my life as a Christian and would recommend that anyone who wants to dive deeper into the waters of their faith, reach out and discern a good spiritual director. Having a director to guide you and help find where God is active in your prayer life is the life buoy in the deep waters of faith to guide you safely home.

Seminary Experience

Without a doubt, I believe that I would not be the person I am today had I not attended Sacred Heart Major Seminary in Detroit, Michigan. From the very first time I entered the building to meet with an admissions director until the last class I took before moving out of Michigan, I was mesmerized with the holiness of the seminary and the people that lived, prayed, studied, and taught there. For the first time in my life, I was in a place where it was okay to talk about my faith, to raise questions about what I understood about God, and to get answers to all the questions I had asked myself for so many years, basically my whole life.

I was surrounded with many other lay students like myself. Lay students are people, both men and women, who are living the vocation of their life as married or single persons, not in religious life. The laity, as they are referred to in the Catholic church, are 99 percent of the 1.3 billion Catholics in the world. There would be no church without religious monks and sisters and priests to administer the sacraments, but so too, there would be no church without the laity doing the heavy lifting of fund raising, teaching, volunteering, and sharing the faith through their lives and actions.

I was amazed to see so many professional people taking time from their busy schedules to attend classes and deepen their faith. I was especially astounded to see all the young men that were attending the seminary in priestly formation. Typically, between nineteen and twenty-five, these young men were absolutely alive with their faith. At a time when many young men are trying to figure out what they want to do with their lives and hanging out with buddies and playing video games, all of which is normal and not a knock against them, these young seminarians were instead pursuing their faith in the most dedicated of ways. These men were committing themselves to a life of celibacy and serving others throughout their lives. I was and still am impressed by the dedication to their faith that these young men have.

The seminarians that I met came from various family upbringings and different life experiences. Some were college ball players, had considered a professional career in computers or accounting but instead chose to follow God when they heard that persistent small voice in the back of their heads. Because of their faith, they had left everything they knew behind to pursue something they likely knew very little about.

The seminary in Detroit is located near the historic Boston Edison District. In the tumultuous times of the mid to late 1960s, the seminary's location placed it near the center of the riots in Detroit. After the riots had taken place, and tenuous calm had come back to the area, one of the locals came to the seminary and painted the Jesus statue that sat on the front lawn. It was no act of common vandalism, but the local resident instead painted the face of Jesus black. Almost immediately many in the seminary went out to "clean up" the statue and restore it to its original all-white finish. Fortunately, someone in charge at the seminary had the wisdom to make the following decision: If the community that we live in see Jesus as a black man, who are we to change Him back to our idealized image of him. To this day, more than fifty years later, the black Jesus still stands on the ground of Sacred Heart Major Seminary as a tribute to the local residents who had the courage to challenge the status quo and to the seminary leadership who were inspired enough to see the wisdom in this.

Studies of Different Faiths

"Be very careful if you are thinking of doing yoga," my paternal grandmother warned me when I was in my thirties. I was a goalie on a hockey team and felt that yoga would be a tremendous benefit for me in stretching and overall flexibility to prevent me from becoming injured. "Be careful what teacher you go to and only do the postures. Don't start chanting and other things that aren't Catholic," I was warned. Being young and immature in my faith, I was often wary of dialoging with those of other faiths. Either they would ask me questions about my faith and expose me as a fraud, or they would try to convert me, or so I was told, and I did not want to deal with that.

As I grew in my understanding of my faith, I became more and more comfortable with it and felt secure in my knowledge and understanding of God's unconditional love for me. I also learned, very importantly, that it was also okay to say I don't know when asked a question about my faith. In addition, I was deeply intrigued by other faiths and came to enjoy asking others about their beliefs. I was no longer worried about drifting away from my faith and thus remaining isolated within my walls of doubt but felt free to ask and explore to seek understanding. I wasn't looking or afraid of being converted, and I wasn't looking to change others' minds about their faiths. If someone saw my faith and the happiness I had from it and wanted to know about it, I would happily share. Living my faith as an example was what I felt comfortable with and not so much with evangelizing. I have many friends that do street evangelization. Street evangelization is where they set up a little table on a street corner and hand out rosaries and share their faith. I have tremendous respect and admiration for these friends who share their faith in this way. They are taking the example of the apostles and going out in pairs to spread the faith. I have tried this and found it not to be my charism. The quiet contemplation of a more monastic type of life is where I find God and where He speaks to me.

As my faith matured and I became more confident in it, I actively pursued discussions with my friends of different faiths to better understand their beliefs. Often, almost always actually, how they understood and lived their faith was drastically different than how it was portrayed by the media in the United States. Even, sadly, many Catholics I have met have held a quiet bias against those of different faiths. In my travels, studies, and discussions, I have learned so much from my friends of different faiths. They have helped me grow in my own faith and as a person. I am forever indebted to my Muslim, Hindu, Jain, and Buddhist friends. The quiet stillness of Buddhism has helped me in my meditation and centering prayer practices. The submission of my Muslim friends to the faith of Islam has strengthened my ardor for the renunciation of many things in my life as a Christian. The chanting and mystical prayer of my Sufi friends has helped me in my charismatic prayer and being open to the gifts of the Holy Spirit. Finally, the strict adherence to the ardent nonviolence of the Jain monks I prayed with has helped me better understand Jesus command to love thy neighbor as thy self, to turn the other cheek, and that the meek shall inherit the earth.

Two books that helped me tremendously on this path of understanding of the points of convergence in all major faiths were *The Rule of St. Benedict, A Commentary in light of World Ascetic Traditions*, by Mayeul de Dreuille, OSB, and *Benedict's Dharma: Buddhists Reflect on the Rule of Saint Benedict* by Patrick Henry. As I read these amazing books, I became deeply interested in the shared ascetic practices of my Benedictine spirituality and Buddhism and Hinduism especially. Much of the same quiet interior life that St. Benedict writes about is similar in nature to what Buddhists refer to when they speak of enlightenment and letting go. Often as Christians when we go to our inner room and pray quietly, we think of God and try to thank Him for our many blessings and occasionally just be quiet, meditate, and listen for His reply. In Buddhism, when I have joined Buddhist meditation groups, we often would attempt to clear our minds of all thoughts and let go of all attachments. There was no creator God we were praying to, but the same quieting of my mind that I practiced with my Buddhist friends was absolutely invaluable in my attempts to quiet my mind and listen for God. I had started to write that we would *simply* attempt to clear our minds of all thoughts, but for anyone who has tried to meditate for even a short amount of time, you know that trying to clear your mind of thoughts is anything but simple. Like any physical exercise, it takes practice to strengthen that muscle. Buddhism has taught me much about quieting my mind, detachment from material things, and calmness. I have found that none of these teachings, when utilized in deepening my connection to God, is contrary to anything I have studied in the Bible or in the Rule of St. Benedict.

Like Christianity, there is not simply one type of Buddhism any more than there is one type of Christian. In Christianity, there are Baptists, Methodists, Lutherans, Catholics, and many, many more. In Buddhism, some of the largest branches are Theravada, Zen, and Mahayana Buddhists. Theravada is the oldest of these practices while Mahayana, or the "Greater Vehicle," is the largest. Throughout the United States, there are many Buddhist temples that welcome visitors to experience their temple and to pray and meditate with them. I have been blessed to visit several of these temples, and I found the monks and the people who lived and prayed there extremely kind and welcoming. While I lived in the St. Louis area, I visited the MABA (Mid-American Buddhist Association) temple in Augusta, Missouri. On one visit, unbeknownst to me when I arrived, it was a special day of prayer to a certain bodhisattva, or enlightened one. In addition to meditating in the temple, we did a meditation walk to the shrine of this bodhisattva. A meditative walk is a wonderful experience and something we can all do each day. We walk slowly while consciously thinking about each step, about the earth beneath our feet, and give thanks for the blessings of that moment. We do not get distracted in thinking about where we are going or what we need to get done when we get there, we simply are present in each footstep. We let our love and the love of creation unite in each step we take. It is a wonderful experience.

During this visit to the Buddhist temple, after walking back and forth to the shrine, we gathered in the temple and did a thirty-minute meditation. We all kneeled on the cushions and mats provided. We were lined up in rows facing the front with ample space between us so that while we were gathered as a large group, there was free space around us to allow us to be comfortable. At the start of the meditation session, a simple bell was rung to signal the start of the session. There was the typical rustling of people getting comfortable, the coughing of people clearing their throats, and the other small, simple things that can distract you from your own meditation if you let them. Instead, the goal is to notice the disturbance and quietly and quickly let it pass from your thoughts. Thus, you return to the quiet, peaceful darkness of the void of thought where you try to think of nothing. My words do not come close to describing the beauty and richness of this practice and the peace and calmness it brings to your soul. Just as you are required to occasionally take a nap to rest your body, meditation is a nap for the mind in which you allow it to rest, regardless of how hard it is. The mind always wants to work and think, and slowing it down shutting it off for even a few moments is a powerful experience of peace.

When meditating with the Buddhists in the Houston community, Tami and I visited a Zen Buddhist center. Here the meditation was a much different experience. Prior to starting, we were asked to sit in the lotus position and the teacher evaluated our posture and position. It was a much more precise and directed meditation. Instead of sitting in rows, facing the front, and meditating with our eyes closed, we sat in a large circle. The circle was outward facing, and we sat with our eyes open and focused on a particular empty space on a nearby wall. The sessions were two twenty-minute sits that were started and ended with the ringing of a small gong that was in the room. I had never meditated in this manner. Sitting in a circle facing outward and focusing on the wall in front of me removed the distraction of the person in front and behind and next to me because they were not there. Meditating with my eyes opened seemed to allow my mind less access to drifting off into thoughts. It was a unique experience for me and showed me just as there is no one way to pray, there are multiple ways to meditate as well. To this day, these experiences of meditating with my Buddhist friends have helped me to learn to control my mind and let go of things much easier. It was a blessing for me to be able to participate in these sessions.

I have written previously about living and working in Egypt, surrounded by the Muslim faith. It was not at all like I had expected based upon what I was taught in the United States. In all my time in Egypt and with all the literally hundreds of people I met, there was only one individual who told me not to ask questions about faith as he did not want to speak about it. Everyone else was open to sharing with me their understanding of Islam, what they had been taught growing up from their Imam and the Koran. They shared with me what they did not believe about Christianity and what they felt to be the truth. I deeply respected that they shared these thoughts with me without saying they must be right, and I must be wrong. It was simply, this is what I believe and why, and then I would tell them what I believed and why. It was an open discussion between friends who respected one another for the depth of their faith. I was deeply moved by their commitment to attaining the five pillars of their faith, of renunciation of physical substance during the period of Ramadan, their dedication to daily prayers, and so much more of the beauty of their faith.

I was once reading a book from someone whom I can't exactly recall, perhaps it was Fr. Bede Griffiths, and he gave an analogy that I thought about and really reflected on. Think of God as your hand. In the palm is God himself. Extending out from the palm are the five major faiths—Christianity, Judaism, Islam, Hinduism, and Buddhism. When the fingers are extended, they are all pointing out in different directions, but at their base, they are all connected to the same palm. Purist of each faith will say they are not related and quickly point out the differences, of which indeed there are many. But if we look deeper for points of connection, we can see that the people who practice these faiths are all connected to the same palm, the same God that created everything and everyone. Sadly, in today's world, this spiritual hand is clenched in the form a fist, ready to strike at anything and anyone that disagrees with each other's ideas. How wonderful it will be when this hand softens its grip and becomes open and welcoming like the hands of our parents as they gently tended to us when we were young.

In the unlikely community of Fenton, Michigan, I was offered the opportunity to be able to pray and chant with a group of Sufis who lived in the area. Sufis are the mystics of the Muslim faith. Like the charismatics and mystics of the Christian faith, I often think that the traditional Muslims don't quite know what to make of these Sufis. If you have ever seen a video of a Sufi whirling dervish, you will quickly realize this is not a traditional Muslim prayer service. The Sufi mystics use the whirling of their bodies to put themselves into a trancelike state that deepens their meditation. Thus, the whirling dervish is a physical prayer to God. Just as noted that there are multiple types of Christianity and Buddhism, so is the case with the faith of Islam. The differences between Sunni and Shia Muslims are well known in the west because of the wars we have seen, and participated in, in Iran and Iraq. Sufis are predominantly Sunni. When I met and chanted with these Muslim mystics, these details were not discussed, but instead it was recognition of thanks to God that we both shared and focused on.

When we met at a friend's house in Fenton for these chanting sessions with the Sufis, there were typically twenty to thirty people present. We would often meet for meditation sessions, and when the Sufis joined us, it was a special day. The Sufis would join us in meditation, but then upon completion, we would join them in chanting. The chanting was in Arabic and took on a very rhythmic, trancelike quality as we chanted for many minutes. In retrospect, I look back on this experience as a great way to connect with others of different faiths in the language they used to communicate with God.

As I was studying different faiths for a class in world religions at the seminary, one faith kept coming up in my studies as a very interesting religion and one that seemed to speak to me—Jainism. I really had no experience or interactions with any Jains previous to that point in my life. In the area I was raised in Michigan, and perhaps in most of the Midwest, there were no Jain communities to interact with. As I studied the different faiths however, the extreme emphasis on nonviolence that Jains practice really intrigued me. In a culture now where it is difficult to go a day without hearing of violence and killing by simply turning on the TV or looking at your phone, the Jain approach to not harming any living creature really resonated with me.

Jainism is an ancient religion from many millennia before Christianity. Formed in India, it is a nontheistic religion, which is a fancy way of saying that Jains do not believe in an all powerful creator God like Judaism and Christianity and Islam does. The Jains I met were very kind and preached a harmony between man and nature. As those who wish to harm no creatures, they were, of course, vegans.

As I was nearing the end of my full-time work career, I was looking for a way to burn most of my vacation time before I retired. Living near St. Louis at the time, I found a Jain Ashram, or retreat center, located in northern Texas. The selections of Jain retreat centers in the United States is a bit limited, and this center seemed very nice from the research I did on the Internet. So, with a week to spend, my wife and I got in our car and drove to Texas for a weeklong retreat at Siddhayatan Jain retreat center. Both my wife and I had wanted to start a fast to sort of reboot our dietary and health choices, and staying with the Jains seemed like a great time. Jains are known for their ascetic practices, and they had an excellent program for those who were fasting and a simple meal plan for when you ended your fast.

After checking into the center, we were led to a simple room with two twin beds that would be our home for the week. It was not unlike other retreat centers I had stayed in with the exception that there were no religious images or crucifixes on the wall. There was a program put together for prayers and chanting in the morning and evening. Yoga was offered to those participants who wanted to pay a little extra. Mostly it was a quiet time with no TVs or phones and silence expected for most of the time. I greatly enjoyed my time at this retreat center and completed a ten-day fast while I was there. I had started my fast before we left, and I ended it while I was there so I would have their help reintroducing solid foods back into my diet.

During the time I stayed at this retreat, we would hear a short talk from the spiritual master of the center, Acharya Shree Yogeesh.

Acharya is considered to be an enlightened master by the members of his community, and indeed, he spoke with a wisdom and presence that was palpable. His teachings made good sense to me about nonviolence and vegetarianism and detachment from material things. Acharya and his community seemed to me to be kind and peaceful, and though I didn't share the core beliefs of their faith, I felt I was enriched by my time there, and it led me closer to the teachings of Jesus regarding love and respect for all others.

I am blessed to have had these opportunities to live and study with so many people of different faiths than mine. These experiences have helped shape me into the man of faith that I have become. They have strengthened my faith and not diluted or made me question it. I can see the power of God in the lives of all people regardless of what name they give Him.

Thomas Merton and Bede Griffith

I have found throughout my life that the more I learn about a subject, the more I am intrigued to continue to dig deeper on the topic. My study of scripture and of how to live my faith was no different. I became a voracious reader of mystical and spiritual writers of our time and throughout history. From authors such as Thomas Aquinas, St. Augustine, G. K. Chesterton, I found a treasure trove of writings about the faith I was learning about. As I read many great novels of western civilization, books from two authors kept coming up as references from other authors. These two authors were both born in Europe in the early twentieth century and came to Catholicism after their teenage years. Both had interesting conversion stories and became ardent followers of the faith, eventually becoming priests and monks. Thomas Merton was born in 1915 in France and, after studying in England, moved to America where he would become one of the greatest and most prodigious spiritual writers of the twentieth century. Merton was a Cistercian monk who studied and wrote volumes about Eastern religions as well as his own Catholic faith. Bede Griffiths was born in 1906 in England and later become a Benedictine monk. Fr. Griffith lived in India for the last half of his life and was a noted Yogi and interfaced extensively with those of the Hindu faith. I think what attracted me to these writers was their desire to find a common bond between their Catholic faith and the faiths of Hinduism, Buddhism, and Taoism.

I would say that I have read more works of Thomas Merton than likely any other writer. There is a wonderful book entitled *The Hidden Ground of Love*, which is a collection of Thomas Merton's correspondence with many notable figures of his time. These letters are open and frank and discuss his questions about his own beliefs, politics, religion, society, the Vietnam war, and many other topics. As a Cistercian monk, Merton was not able to leave the monastery very often, and yet he had an amazing number of friends with which whom he corresponded with. These letters when read over the course of his life with a perspective now about what was going on in society are powerful and prophetic. Merton was an ardent advocate of nonviolence and was vehemently opposed to the war in Vietnam and most especially nuclear weapons. Many of his writings in this book were collected at the height of the Cold War era between the United States and the Soviet Union. Rhetoric was heated and hateful, and it was about domination and destruction. Merton wanted neither and sought a more peaceful path. He was devastated at the murders of the Kennedys and Martin Luther King and so many other civil rights advocates of his time. His writing is raw with passion, grace, wit, and intellect and moved me deeply. As I was reading this book, I felt like I was participating in his private conversations with so many people I have read about.

When I got to a point later in my life where I chose to downsize and move out of the large house and the acquisition of expensive and unnecessary goods, I had to get rid of a large number of my books. I had thousands of books, and though I hardly ever went back and read a book I had finished, they felt like they were a part of who I was. I struggled mightily to decide which books to keep and which ones to donate. Without hesitation however, all my books from Merton immediately went to the "must keep" box. I reread his books, listened to his lectures on my phone, and kept most everything I have related to Merton. Though he died just a few years after I was born, he is my, and I'm sure many other seekers, posthumous spiritual director. He has helped me in so many ways as I have navigated my own questions of faith. His teachings and lectures that he gave to the novices at Gethsemane are timeless, and I learn something from them each time I listen to them.

Fr. Bede Griffiths was the other author whose works spoke to me as I read them. His most famous book, *The Golden String*, his autobiography, was eye-opening to me. By the time I had read this book, I was a Benedictine oblate and knew a fair amount about Benedictine spirituality. To see Fr. Bede seek to join two of the largest religions in the world, Catholicism and Hinduism into a congruent spirituality was quite interesting to me. There were, of course, critics on each side of these faiths who felt that Fr. Bede was not seeking to just find a common point of these faiths but was instead subverting both religions. To me, Fr. Bede was stretching what was acceptable to many Catholics and Hindus while pushing to highlight what is good and holy in both faiths. This spoke to me as I also sought to find these points of convergence. I never sought to diminish my faith for the elevation of another, but so many teachings I have studied in all these different faiths point back to *love* as the key. How this is expressed and how it is taught and communicated may be different, but *love* is at the root of many faiths. To watch Fr. Bede in old interviews on the Internet and read his books, I saw a kind, gentle, and loving person. A Benedictine monk who dressed in Hindu garb and actually adorned his crucifix with an Om symbol was someone I wanted to learn more about.

As my faith matured, I came to learn that the more I thought I knew, the less I realized I really understood. Knowledge without wisdom can be very dangerous. As I read the novels written by these men, I came to realize that as brilliant and faithful as they were, they too were seeking wisdom throughout their entire lives. They had completed years of rigorous academic studies at prestigious colleges, and yet, in the end, they sought truth from the simple relationships they had with others and with God. Their striving to learn and find common grounds helped me as I matured in my faith and served as compass points for me as I navigated my spiritual journey.

Silent Retreats

As I continued to study and mature my faith, I was spending more and more time seeking silence to both pray and to listen. I was blessed to live near Manresa Jesuit retreat center. This Jesuit retreat house offers chances nearly every week for group retreats or individual retreats. As with most Jesuit houses, silence is both prized and expected when staying at the house. Silence fosters a sense of reflection and allows everyone in the house quiet time away from all the distractions of our daily lives.

As with most things in my life, moderation was not something I was very good at, so for my first attempt at a retreat, I decided I would do an individual self-directed weeklong retreat. I didn't really know what to expect other than that I would have a good opportunity to pray. As I was always busy at work, having a few quite moments would be a welcome respite from my daily routine. I quickly found out that a week of silence was far more than a few moments, and on the first day, I was overwhelmed with the thought of what I would do to fill my time for the next week. It took me several days to find a rhythm of prayer, silence, attending mass, and most surprising, taking a nap. I have never been able to take naps. My mind runs, and I lay in bed thinking about all the stuff I could and should be doing, and after about fifteen minutes of mentally beating myself up for being lazy, I jump out of bed and find something to keep me busy. At Manresa, there was nothing else I had to do. I figured why not read some scripture, pray about it, and maybe drift off for a short nap. It was wonderful. I was able to slow my mind and my body down for that short time and really just be present with and for God. It was perhaps my first look ahead of what life after work might look like. Nothing so pressing I couldn't take time for myself and my faith.

When I arrived that first week, I was ready to get holy and wanted to get there quickly. I figured I would go straight to hard-core asceticism and fast the entire week. By the end of the week, I figured I would emerge enlightened both mentally and physically. I would likely leave the retreat house with the priests there wondering how they too could become so holy. I quickly learned that my idea of holiness and how to get there didn't necessarily line up with the priest I was assigned to talk to once each day. His first advice to me was, maybe don't fast. For my first experience for a retreat like this, I would spend the bulk of the days worrying about the growling in my stomach, and I would be distracted from having a true spiritual experience. Luckily, I was smart enough to listen to his wise advice and figured I would only eat a small amount each meal, and I could still emerge at the end of the week holier than when I started. After my first home-cooked meal there by the staff of cooks, I figured it would be best just to eat normal as God wouldn't be providing such delicious food if he didn't want me to eat it. Since then, I have fasted numerous times, but I am so glad I listened to Fr. Peter and did not try that for my first retreat experience.

Since then, I have had many silent retreats of varying length, and I find them to be absolutely beneficial in resetting my compass toward true north. I can get turned around in the field of my own thoughts and what I prioritize, and these retreats help to reset the compass and ensure I am on the right path. If you have not done one of these, don't hesitate to take this time for yourself. Find a good retreat house with good spiritual directors and invest some time in the most important investment you have, your physical and spiritual well-being.

CHAPTER 12
Benedictine Spirituality and Balance

> *Benedictine spirituality is the spirituality of the twenty-first century because it deals with the issues facing us now."*
> —Joan Chittister, OSB

Benedict and His Rule

The day was coming to a close, and she had enjoyed the day with her brother. They had walked among the gardens near the home they had both visited and talked about family life and life in their respective communities. Each of them lived in a large community of people, and yet, as twins, they shared a special connection as siblings that went beyond words. Though they lived only five miles apart, the countryside and traditions of sixth century Italy precluded them from spending a lot of time together. But this was a special night, and the sister was not eager for her brother to leave.

"Let's just stay and talk a bit longer," she said to him insistently.

Equally resolved, he replied, "Sister, it has been a blessing to spend this day together sharing a good meal, discussing all of the blessings the Lord has given us, and walking through the countryside, but I really must return home. My brothers will be waiting for me."

Quietly, the sister bowed her head and joined her hands in quiet prayer as they sat around the table in the dining room of the small cabin they were in. Almost instantly, the sky darkened, and thunder crashed and echoed against the walls of the mountains that surrounded them. Lighting tore through the darkness of the night, illuminating the torrents of rain that had just as quickly started to fall. "My dear sister, what have you done?" the brother replied in wonderment.

"I asked you to stay, and you would not listen," she replied to her awestricken brother. "So I asked the Lord, and He did," she said as a sly, yet pious smile slowly formed on her face. "If you still feel you need to leave, feel free to venture into the darkness and the rain," she suggested to her brother.

"Sister, I do not wish to anger the Lord, or you for that matter," he said cautiously as the storm raged on. "I will stay, and we will continue to spend the evening together." Thus, the final meeting between St. Scholastica and St. Benedict, twin siblings born in the late fifth century carried on through the night and into the early sunrise of the next morning.

Finally leaving for home, fully enjoying the sacred time he had spent with his sister, St. Benedict returned to the monastic community he had formed. They had spent the night speaking of spiritual matters and praying for themselves and their communities. It was not more than three days later when Benedict had a vision in his sleep of his sister, now passing away into eternity and her soul flying from her body, in the shape of a white dove, up to the heavens and God's embrace.

Greif stricken, St. Benedict sent some of the other monks to the adjacent monastery where St. Scholastica lived to console her community and bring her body back to His monastery. Overwhelmed with sadness at the passing of his sister, he had her body buried in the tomb that had been specially created for him. Four years later, when he too left this earth to share with his sister in the beatific vision of God's face, he left instructions for his community to bury him in the same tomb as his sister so their earthly remains would remain forever together until they were raised from the dead on the last day.

It is this loving spirituality of brother and sister that has help guide my spiritual growth nearly fifteen centuries later. St. Benedict created the manuscript for monastic life that is read daily to this day by those living in religious communities. The Rule of St. Benedict was largely taken from an early writing entitled *The Rule of the Master* written by an unknown author.

The brilliance of the Rule of St. Benedict was the way in which he took the original rule and added and deleted content to make his new *rule* much more forgiving of the human condition in which we all struggle with. By adding the love of a father to the original rule and yet keeping the strictness of much of the original intentions, Benedict crafted a set of guidelines that I read daily to help me in my struggles as a father, a husband, and a leader at work. I had attended an oblate directors' conference at St. Scholastica Monastery in Duluth, Minnesota, and one of the speakers there, a Benedictine sister, from a local community postulated that the tender qualities of the rule came not directly from Benedict but from those long discussions with his sister St. Scholastica. While I am not sure of the accuracy of this, I am also not sure it is not entirely true. The tempering of the original rule of the master seems to have a feminine, loving, and caring quality about it. So, the supposition that Scholastica helped her brother write the *rule* seems as likely to be true as it is a fabrication of someone's imagination.

The beauty of the *rule* as it applies to me and my life is the strictness to teachings of the Lord and the tenderness to those we live and love. Don't be confused, the *rule* is no touchy-feely set of instructions that are easy to look at and chose to follow or not. In fact, they seemed so strict to some members of Benedict's community, those that had lived a monastic life without boundaries prior to entering his community, that they sought to poison St. Benedict and kill him so they could live a life less structured and centered on God. Whenever you see a religious statue of a monk with a bird at his foot carrying a piece of bread in his mouth, that figure is St. Benedict. It is said a raven was sent from God to pick up and remove the poisoned bread from Benedict before he could eat it. Additionally, his wine had also been poisoned, and when he blessed the cup of wine prior to drinking it, the cup shattered in pieces, spilling the deadly drink and thwarting his erstwhile brothers in their attempts of slacker subterfuge.

The Rule of St. Benedict has seventy-three chapters, and they discuss everything one needs to know while living in community. Many of the chapters are, for me, unbearably detailed in how to conduct the smallest parts of our lives and our prayers. The prologue to the *Rule*, chapter 7 on "Humility," and other key chapters however speak to me with a clarity that resounds like a bell. That these words written 1,500 years ago are still so relevant and true is in itself a miracle and leads me to believe it was indeed inspired writing, or maybe just good sisterly advice.

To be truthful, when I was living and working in the corporate world, I was not faithful to reading the *rule* on a daily basis. There are all sorts of online versions of the *rule* and even translations that give you a day by day guide for what part to read. For example, open to the book to the current date, and you will find a short section just for that day. The readings are usually no more than a paragraph or a few lines. The *rule* is not meant to be read chapter after chapter and then reflected upon certain key points. Instead, it is meant to be taken in small sections and reflected deeply upon each lesson. Often I would find myself reading multiple days of the rule instead of just the single paragraph. "That's it?" I would find myself asking. Only after time did I start to grasp the depth and full meaning of these small slices of wisdom.

Only when I spent time living as a volunteer in community at Mount St. Scholastica, a women's Benedictine community in Atchison, Kansas, did I faithfully read from the rule each day. The prioress would read from the rule at the start of morning prayer and would then read a reflection from a fellow Benedictine monastic or a Benedictine oblate. So often, the section of the *rule* that Sr. Esther would read had an immediate correlation to something I was dealing with in my daily life. Timeless in its teaching and powerful in the lessons it provides, the Rule of St. Benedict has helped form me into who I am today.

Oblate Life

From their website, the Benedictine sisters of Baltimore describe nicely what it is to be an oblate of St. Benedict,

> Oblates are everyday people with jobs, families, and other responsibilities. They come from a variety of faith traditions. In today's hectic, changing world, being an oblate offers a rich spiritual connection to the stability and wisdom of an established monastic community. By their commitment to the Rule of Benedict, oblates benefit from an ancient spiritual tradition that has led countless other monastics and oblates to holiness. Just as a candidate for the monastery is tested to see whether they "truly seeks God" (RB 58), so also those who become oblates are committed above all else to seek God in Jesus Christ. (https://www.emmanuelosb.org/oblates.html)

For me, when I was searching for a way to deepen my faith and learn from people who had taken the journey I was looking to embark on, finding a Benedictine oblate community was critical in my faith formation. This is not a radical change to one's life where you must give up your possessions, join a monastery, shave your head, and learn Karate. No, on the contrary, it is a gentle shift in one's priorities to help orient us more from the world we live in, to the community we desire to join when we die.

All of the Benedictine monasteries handle their oblate meetings just a bit differently. Some meet monthly, some weekly, and some only a few times a year. Some meetings are held on Saturdays and include attending prayers and mass with the community at the monastery while others are on Sundays and include attending community mass with the brothers or sisters. Oblate programs are a part of both monasteries with religious sisters, nuns, or men monastics. The oblate directors, those that guide the meetings and generally set the agenda for the discussions, have typically been professed religious members of the community. This means either a priest, a brother, or a nun. Recently, there has been an increasing trend to look at lay members of the community to be the director. The beauty of the *rule* and the oblate community is that either-or is correct. The Benedictine spirituality of the oblates are not strictly defined by a rigid set of rules or requirements. Thus, after I had spent my novitiate year in studies at St. Benedict monastery in Oxford, Michigan, a community or nine or ten religious brothers and priests and then made my final oblation, my wife, Tami, decided that this life and spirituality was for her as well, and she entered the oblate program. Male monastic communities are open to both male and female oblate members just as communities of nuns, religious sisters, have oblate communities comprised of both men and women. It really is the oblate's choice of which monastic community they feel speaks to them and shares their spirituality and the community's decision if this person would make a good oblate.

St. Benedict Monastery

St. Benedict Monastery in Oxford, Michigan, was a hidden gem near the area I had grown up. Growing up Catholic, I was not familiar with monks and monasteries and had no idea that there were several communities with forty-five minutes of where I had spent my formative years. Originally centered at St. Scholastica Monastery in Detroit, the community moved to Oxford, about thirty miles north of Detroit, in the 1950s when the expanding city of Detroit was closing in on them in their original location.

The Benedictine community in Oxford belongs to the Sylvestrine Congregation. This means that they were formed when St. Sylvester Guzzolini adapted the Benedictine rule in the thirteenth century to include a ministry of preaching and pastoral care to the community in which they lived. Part of my novitiate year was spent learning about St. Sylvester and his gifts and how they applied to my life. There are numerous different men and women Benedictine communities in the United States. The largest congregation on the men's side is the American-Cassinese Congregation. Other men congregations include the Swiss-American federation and the Subiaco-Cassinese federation. All are Benedictine, but each has a slightly different flavor or charism. On the women's side, there is the Federation of St. Scholastica, the Federation of St. Benedict, and the Federation of St. Gertrude the Great, to name just the larger ones. Again, though different in their federations, many share much of the same ideology and beliefs.

When I applied at St. Benedict's Monastery in Oxford to become an oblate, I was intrigued by the idea of a group of men living in community and staying faithful to their religious vows. There were younger monks who seemed like colleagues to me and older monks who seemed more fatherly. Having not grown up with much a father figure in my house, I was drawn to the paternal aspects of this community. I would often join the community for morning mass on my way to work and enjoyed building a relationship with the brothers in community. I started to learn much more about what monastic life looks like and how they orient their lives around prayer and work. St. Benedict of Oxford was my first experience with monastic community, and it helped me to discover how my faith could permeate all aspects of my life.

Mount St. Scholastica

Different in so many ways from my first monastic experience, Mount St. Scholastica was a community of Benedictine sisters located in Atchison, Kansas. Originally formed in the late 1800s, the community grew in size in the middle of the twentieth century to include more than six hundred sisters spread out across daughter houses around the United States. The term "daughter house" is the name for a community that is formed when the larger *mother house*, the base of the community, grows such that certain members start a new community elsewhere to share their spirituality in a new location. As the Mount, as it is lovingly referred to, grew to such huge numbers, the prioress sent sisters to different locations around the United States, Brazil, and elsewhere to expand and establish the community around the world.

When I transferred jobs at General Motors and relocated from Michigan to the St. Louis area, one of my fellow Michigan oblates gave me a book entitled *Atchison Blue*, written by Judith Valente. A wonderfully written book, Atchison Blue describes in words, actually paints a beautiful visual image, the beauty that is so present at the Mount. As my wife, Tami, and I were not able to find an oblate community near to where we lived in the St. Louis area, we found the Mount through the book *Atchison Blue* and started attending oblate meetings as visiting oblates. We immediately fell in love with the community in general and the oblate director at the Mount, Sr. Thomasita. Kind, caring, intelligent with a razor-sharp wit, Sr. Thomasita made us feel so welcome as we visited for the first time. My wife loved the community as it felt much warmer to her as a woman. Having 125 religious sisters in community certainly made my wife feel more at home than she had in the small man's community we belonged to in Michigan. To see other women her age living religious life was as eye-opening to my wife as experiencing the monastery in Michigan was to me.

I too enjoyed the community at the Mount. The sisters were very kind, and with it being such a large and older community, the average age is likely in the seventies; there were wonderful stories aplenty when joining the sisters for meals or talking with them in the halls of the monastery. As I was especially close to my maternal grandmother as I grew up and as I took her to church as she neared the end of her life, I saw much of the same faithfulness, wisdom, and strength in these sisters as I had seen in my beloved grandmother.

The campus at the Mount was vast and sprawling; there were acres of trees and rolling hills with many buildings, retreat centers, and volunteer houses. It seemed to me to be massive on a scale I had never experienced in a religious community. The oblate community was equally as large, and attending the meetings, we met many people from across different spectrums of age and spirituality. There seemed to be far more women in the oblate group at the Mount than there had been in Michigan, so this was a learning experience for me as well. Throughout my life, the bulk of my religious influences had been from women, so this very much put me in my comfort zone.

Later on in life, as I decided to step away from the corporate world and pursue my faith even more deeply, the Mount would play a significant role in my life. I had made these first connections through my oblate life, and the seeds that had been planted would come to harvest just a few years later.

CHAPTER 13
A Marriage of Equals

It takes three to make love, not two: you, your spouse, and God. Without God people only succeed in bringing out the worst in one another. Lovers who have nothing else to do but love each other soon find there is nothing else. Without a central loyalty life is unfinished.
—Venerable Fulton Sheen

A Final Chance at Love

Having been in numerous relationships and one long marriage, all of which ended the same way, with me feeling I had failed in the relationship, I was not sure I would ever get into another relationship again. I had separated from my fiancée Judy after I had divorced Lori, my wife of twenty-two years, and felt that through my own choices, bad luck, or my inability to be a good partner, I was not destined to be in a serious relationship with another person. I had decided that perhaps the religious life was for me, and I started to attend workshops that were the very beginning stages of discernment to a religious life as a priest or a monk. Through all the ups and downs of my life, the one person who had loved me unconditionally and who had always been there for me was God. I know it sounds cliché, but it gave me great comfort knowing that regardless of the infinite number of bad decisions I had made, God loved me for me, though even He probably shook his head on some of the choices I had made.

I think that He loved me so much that he allowed me one final chance at a loving and healthy relationship. I had been corresponding with a female friend about mentoring her son as he was entering his teenage years. This friend was someone I had known for nearly fifteen years. In fact, she almost felt like part of my family. This was for good reason.

Tami entered my life seriously after I had been on my own for some time. I had divorced Lori, the subsequent relationship I had with Judy had ended, and I was living on my own for the first time in decades. I had known Tami since she was in her early twenties. My adopted father had remarried after he divorced my mother. When he remarried, his new wife and he had a son together. Though this young man was no blood relationship to me, I always considered him like a brother, though he was much younger than me. I would occasionally visit my dad's house and play with my brother, and though we weren't exceeding close due to the age difference and the limited amount of time I saw him, I still referred to him as my brother.

Over the years as I grew up and got married and moved out of state, I saw less and less of my dad, his new wife, and my brother. My brother was and is a very intelligent person, and because his parents spent a lot of time at work, he had to grow up fast, and he matured at a young age. In the years I was raising my children and married to Lori, I might see my brother once a year at Christmas or sometimes not at all as he had become a police officer and often worked the excessive overtime hours that police are offered and sometimes required to work. My brother would often work Christmas Eve and Christmas day, so I might go years without seeing him. As I grew up and moved away, he grew up and got into a relationship with a woman he had met through friends. Though they never married, they spent several years together and even had two children, a boy and, less than a year later, a baby girl, Irish twins. Their relationship ended shortly after their daughter was born.

Because of my brother's ex-girlfriend's desire to keep their children connected to their father's family, she would often still attend the family Christmas party on Christmas Eve if he couldn't make it, and she would bring the children so they could spend Christmas time with their grandparents. It was always nice to see her and the kids and catch up on how they were all doing. Their son and daughter were only five or six years younger than my sons, so they kids would play together, and it was great for the grandparents to see all the grandkids together.

Fast-forward fifteen years, and it was this ex-girlfriend, who was still single after that and a few other relationships, that connected with me about mentoring her son, my brother's son. As I was helping to coach my youngest son's high school wrestling team at the time, I was more than happy to spend time with her son, my nephew of sorts, and help him with sports and weightlifting and other guy-type activities. It was through this relationship that I became much closer friends with his mother, my brother's ex-girlfriend, Tami. We would continue developing our friendship to the point that we asked each other, "Should we start dating?"

There was the understandable confusion about the legitimacy of dating and entering into a relationship together. Though her children's father was in no way related to me by blood, I had known him since he was born. Though they had been separated for nearly fifteen years and never communicated with each other, what were the boundaries of an acceptable relationship? We struggled with this for some time, and in the end, it caused a rift that exists to this day between my brother and me. I spoke with my brother openly when I started to have feelings for Tami and asked him if he was okay with me dating her. Though I love my brother for our shared life experiences, he was deeply upset that I had developed feelings for his ex-girlfriend. In the end however, Tami and I felt very strongly we had a unique connection that we wanted to explore further.

As we started dating, I wanted to try something totally different than any other relationship I had been in, all of which eventually had fallen apart. I told Tami that as I had walked further into my faith, I felt that to be true to myself and my beliefs, I did not feel that we should engage in premarital sex. We would spend the next year or so or however long the dating relationship would last getting to know each other for who we were and not mix sex into the relationship. I had seen in the past how a strong physical connection could skew my true perspective on the viability of the relationship, and if this was going to get serious, I wanted to know that it was because we cared and respected each other's ideas and beliefs and not just because how we made each other feel physically.

This was a tough call for me and perhaps for Tami as well. We had been in previous long-term relationships; we were not getting any younger and were both very attracted to each other. I felt however this abstinence from premarital sex was absolutely critical to any chance of being in a successful long-term relationship. I prayed often to God during the time I was dating Tami. "God," I said, "I will refrain from my physical desires to honor you and your teachings to love and respect a person for who they are and not for how they make you feel." I had recently read a seminal work by Karol Wojtyla entitled *Love and Responsibility*. There was also a book by Dr. Edward Sri entitled *Men, Women and the Mystery of Love* that broke down Wojtyla's work into more practical terms in such a way that a man of my mental prowess could understand. These books really did change my life and my perspective on what real love is, how a relationship should be formed and nurtured, and the role of sex in a relationship. I tried my best, with the help of daily prayer and God's intercessions, to keep my relationship with Tami within the bounds of these guidelines.

It turned out to be one of the best decisions I had ever made. After a year or so of dating, Tami and I decided to marry. I asked her recently if she remembers how I proposed, I had to ask because I couldn't recall it clearly myself. She informed me that I never really formally proposed. I just told her when we had only been dating for a few months that we were going to get married. I don't necessarily recall this, but it sounds like it could be accurate as pretty quickly I felt a very strong spiritual connection with her.

Tami was a single mom, and due to the children's dad's work schedule, he didn't see the kids a lot. Between working and raising kids, Tami stayed pretty busy. What I was most impressed with was the calm and restrained way in which she raised and disciplined her children. There was not the yelling or physical discipline that I had experienced growing up and that I myself had used to raise my children. There were boundaries set and repercussions when the children did not respect the boundaries. In her life, Tami had come in contact with many people who were familiar with the twelve-step process, and she herself had come to know these practices and teachings very well. She utilized these steps in her daily life and helped me to learn about boundaries and what it meant to be absolutely truthful. For example, in the past, I could talk around a situation without ever directly lying, but also not be totally truthful. If I just omitted parts of the story that I could not say without lying, I could justify to myself that I was being honest. In this relationship however, we both made it clear that to be successful, there could be none of these half-truths and total honesty and respect was required.

I also found out through our relationship that Tami was very much devoted to social justice issues, taking care of oneself through making time for self-care, enjoyed being in nature, and was deeply spiritual in her own way. All of things were extremely attractive to me as a partner, and after finding out that we shared so many common traits, we really couldn't see a reason why not to take our dating further and enter into the sacramental bond of marriage. Again, there came the time for us to share this news with our family. Instead of making a grand announcement, we were cautious of how to share the news so as not to hurt my brother's feelings and wondered how the family would take it. In the end, we reflected that this was a small moment in time, and if we truly had found in each a partner that we would hopefully spend the next forty years together with, it would be foolish not to pursue the relationship further.

After first telling out children of our plans and asking them how they felt about it and if they had questions or concerns, they didn't, we shared the news with a larger audience. In general, the family on my mother's side was very happy and said they had kind of thought this was going to happen. The feelings were mixed on my father's side and on some of Tami's side as well as they had obviously known the children's father. Overall we were relieved to finally publicly share the news, and we had great support from our friends and our children, the people we loved the most.

The wedding ceremony itself was rather small with less than one hundred people total attending. We got married in the small local Catholic church that we both had attended and had a small a subdued reception in the basement of the church. As neither Tami or I drank alcohol by this time in our lives, it was a happy and joyous occasion, but not an out-of-control reception fueled by alcohol and youth, neither of which we had at this wedding.

We had spent over a year getting to know each other better and had tried to develop our relationship in a way that was consistent with our faith. Though Tami was generally raised Catholic, she did not have a strong church upbringing, but she was completely on board with trying something new for our relationship as she too had experienced her share of relationship failures. I hesitate to call these previous relationships failures, because in each relationship, we have the opportunity to learn from them what we did right and what we did wrong. We can learn what to look for in a partner and how to better understand ourselves. So, it may be more accurate to say that both Tami and I had experienced relationships that did not lead to our ultimate goals of total love and honesty and respect for each other and a potential lifetime of married love.

Typically, creating a blended family is very difficult because of different parenting styles and mixing the children together. For us, that was not a significant issue as my two sons were already on their own and had moved out of the house. When college was done for the summer, they might move back for a few months but were often visiting friends or working, so it was never an issue. Also, since the kids had known of each other since they were born and had seen each other on some holidays and occasionally during summer vacations up north at my father's house, they easily connected and had no real conflicts to overcome.

Since I had taken my father's last name when he adopted me, I shared a common surname with my brother, so Tami's children shared a common last name with my sons. When all of us would go on vacation or I would pick her children up from school, it was relatively seamless since we all had the same last name. Most people that we met through school activities or other events just assumed we were one big family since we all shared the same last name, and everyone seemed to get along so well. I felt truly blessed that God had given me another chance at a loving marital relationship and was so grateful to have such a wonderful family. I was and am really committed to always being honest and trying my best to ensure that this marriage would be successful. I found that the best way to do this was to allow God to always be the uniting force between my wife and me. This marriage was not and would not be an infatuation love like I had experienced when I was a young man and not a relationship based simply upon physical attraction, but a committed relationship with God as the center of life and our marriage.

Christ as the Center of Our Marriage

Anyone that has been through marriage preparation classes through a church has likely heard this message, it is critical to keep God as the center of your relationship. I heard that the first time I was married and never really understood what that meant. Sure, we would try to go to church, and we would try to raise the kids to know about the Bible, but Christ as the center of our marriage? I never really had detailed marriage preparation classes for my first marriage. Because of our desire not to upset our grandparents and get married in the Baptist or Catholic church, we had chosen a Lutheran church, and the marriage preparation was really confined to a couple of meetings of thirty minutes or so where the pastor tried to convince us to come to that church after we got married, we had no intention of doing that, and to make sure we were really ready to be married at the relatively young ages we were.

When Tami and I got married however, we had a series of meetings for marriage preparation with the parish priest that we both knew. We each had to fill out a detailed questionnaire about our likes, dislikes, passions, goals, and beliefs. We met with him independently and together as well. It was the most thorough formal preparation I had ever had prior to entering into a serious, committed relationship. After we had completed the questionnaire, Fr. Dave met with us both together and shared the results of our marriage compatibility test. Lucky for us, we seemed to be a good fit! Fr. Dave shared issues that could be problematic based upon our individual beliefs, and his words rang very true. It wasn't totally surprising what he shared, but it was interesting nonetheless to have our relationship examined from this perspective.

What did and does it mean to keep Christ at the center of my marriage? It means, first off, that it is nearly impossible for the marriage to fail if both couples truly and honestly respect the teachings of the church and the message of Jesus. If we truly love each other as we love ourselves, there is no real way that we can lie or be unfaithful to each other. If I were to lie to my wife or even consider being unfaithful, I would be putting love of myself and my own desires above that of my wife's. Christ teaches that we are to love each other as we love ourselves, and if we do this, it becomes really difficult to even consider consciously doing anything that would cause your partner pain. God is one who unites and not a divider. The truest sense of God is love and communion with Him, and that starts with true, open, and honest communion with yourself and your partner.

All this is not to say that you will not have struggles or difficulties in your marriage if you keep Christ as its center. At the root of this relationship are two people who have come together with each of their own struggles, shortcomings, and issues. My insecurity issues of who I am as a person would continue to manifest themselves throughout the early years of our marriage. This led to jealousy and trust issues at certain times because I always felt that there was someone out there better than me and that I was inferior in some way.

In addition to learning absolute honesty, I also had to learn absolute trust. Trusting that my wife loves me as much as I love her and that we both respect and honor each other was a big steppingstone for me. If I totally opened up my heart again, there was a chance that I would get hurt again. Again, through my faith, I was able to ask God for help in learning to deeply and honestly love and trust another person. Our shared faith is a source of great strength and inspiration for us. While we do each go to church individually when the other's schedule does not permit attendance at the same time, we really always strive to attend together and to share the experience. We will often reflect on the message of the day and how it spoke to us. It is interesting and wonderful to hear how the same message I told was

...imes heard so differently by my wife. Her perspectives are often very unique and helps me to continue to grow and learn.

Twelve Steps to Happiness

The twelve-step program was written by Bill Wilson and Dr. Robert Holbrook Smith in 1935. Nearly a hundred years old, this program has saved the lives of a countless number of lost souls who had lost everything to their varying addictions of drugs, alcohol, gambling, and sex. I was blessed by the fact that Tami was very familiar with these steps, and when we married, I was able to learn and better understand them myself. For those not familiar, the twelve steps developed Bill W. and Dr. Bob as they relate to alcoholism are as follows—

1. We admitted we were powerless over alcohol—that our lives had become unmanageable.
2. Came to believe that a Power greater than ourselves could restore us to sanity.
3. Made a decision to turn our will and our lives over to the care of God as we understood Him.
4. Made a searching and fearless moral inventory of ourselves.
5. Admitted to God, to ourselves, and to another human being the exact nature of our wrongs.
6. Were entirely ready to have God remove all these defects of character.
7. Humbly asked Him to remove our shortcomings.
8. Made a list of all persons we had harmed, and became willing to make amends to them all.
9. Made direct amends to such people wherever possible, except when to do so would injure them or others.
10. Continued to take personal inventory and when we were wrong promptly admitted it.
11. Sought through prayer and meditation to improve our conscious contact with God, as we understood Him,

praying only for knowledge of His will for us and the power to carry that out.
12. Having had a spiritual awakening as the result of these Steps, we tried to carry this message to alcoholics, and to practice these principles in all our affairs.

As you can see from the list above, a belief in God or a higher power is absolutely necessary, in my opinion, for this program to be successful. If have been to many meetings where the term *God* is highly objectionable to some of the attendees, so *Higher Power* is often used as a more comfortable terminology.

Without doing a line by line comparison, it was through my study of my Benedictine spirituality that I discovered the twelve steps of humility in the rule of St. Benedict. Written nearly 1,500 years before the twelve steps program, there are striking similarities between these two twelve steps "programs." Listed below are the twelve steps of humility from the rule of St. Benedict, summarized from https://stbenedict.catholic.org.hk/english/EnglishCommunity/12steps.htm:

Step 1. A first step is taken when one consciously obeys all of God's commandments, never ignoring them but always holding within himself a fear of God in his heart.
Step 2. The second step is achieved when one thinks not about pleasing himself but instead follow the injunction of the Lord.
Step 3. The third step is reached when out of love of God, one obediently submits to a superior in imitation of the Lord.
Step 4. The fourth step is achieved when one, under obedience, patiently and quietly endures all thing that are inflicted on him. It should make no difference whether the trials are painful, unjust or even completely beyond his understanding; he should neither tire nor give up.
Step 5. The fifth step is reached when one humbly discloses to his superior all the evil thoughts in his heart, as well as those faults and evil acts he has actually committed.

Step 6. To achieve the sixth step one must without qualms accept all that is crude and harsh; at all times he considers himself a poor and worthless workman.

Step 7. The seventh step is attained when one not only confesses that he is an inferior and common wretch, but believes it to his very core. He must be willing to humble himself.

Step 8. One reaches the eighth step of humility when he does only that which is demanded by the common rule of his seniors.

Step 9. The ninth step can be achieved when one, practicing silence, only speaks when asked a question.

Step 10. The tenth step is climbed when one restrains himself from undue laughter and frivolity.

Step 11. To reach the eleventh step one must speak gently, without jests, but simply, seriously, tersely, rationally and softly.

Step 12. The final step is attained only when one can at all times show humility not only in his appearance and actions, but also in his heart.

I find the similarities between the two sets of twelve-step guidelines directions to be strikingly similar. In each we must recognize the existence of God, or a higher power, we must then recognize that we are not Him, we are not God. We must lower ourselves in humility or hit "rock bottom" in the twelve-step program before we can begin to rise again. In all things, humility is important. I found this to be absolutely true in marriage as well. When I start to exalt myself over my partner, to feel I am more important to the marriage or doing more than her, that is when I start to have problems. My ego can often get in the way when I begin to value my contributions more than those of my spouse, and that is where the trouble begins. Between the two of us, we have become very familiar with these two twelve-step programs and try to integrate them into our lives and our marriage every day. I am confident that the success of our marriage to this point is in no small part attributable to the fact that these guidelines help direct us each day.

Codependency Issues

Growing up, I subconsciously recognized at a very young age that my role was to be the comedian of the family and to try to get people to laugh to ease the tension. This behavior and the attention and recognition it provided led to an adult life of codependency. I took on the role of trying to solve everyone's issues, even if they did not involve me. Anyone that needed help, I was there to try to solve their problems for them or enable them to continue their behaviors in the name of help.

This behavior especially manifested itself in one of my relationships before I married Tami. Judy had issues with a specific substance, and instead of working with her to resolve the problem, I would often make excuses for her and do things to ease the pain of her choices. In the end, I was not helping her to heal because instead of her experiencing the true ramifications of her decisions, I was there to soften the landing. By doing this, the true impact was not felt by her, and she was not allowed to hit her rock bottom to begin recovery. So, while my intention was to help out of love, I in fact extended these issues for her by my codependent behavior.

It was not until we eventually separated that she was able to be allowed to truly hit her bottom and begin the road to recovery. It was not until I got married to Tami, and I exhibited these same behaviors, that I was called out for them. While my help and concern were appreciated, it was not my place to step in and try to fix things. We cannot make other people heal themselves; they must recognize the issue, want to change, and then do the work themselves. Growing up with many extended family members and friends who had substance abuse issues, I realized the idea to allow them to experience the full consequences of their decisions seemed absolutely foreign to me. I, and other family members as well, would seek to control the damages and the fallout from decisions made by those family members who were struggling to put on the best public face for the family.

It was not until these behaviors began to affect our marriage did Tami recognize them in me and give me advice on how to address them. Firstly, I read a very popular book entitled *Codependent No*

More by Melody Beattie. The stories and advice in here seemed absolutely counterintuitive to me. How could I show someone I truly loved them by letting them fail? Wasn't my job to keep them from making decisions and helping them to fix themselves? These ideas went against everything I thought I understood from growing up in my family of origin.

The second and more powerful step I took to address my codependency issues was that I began to attend Al Anon meetings. In these meetings, I heard heartbreaking stories of parents who had lost their children to drug addiction and those whose marriages had ended when they started to step back and end their codependent behaviors. But beyond that, I heard amazing stories of grace and healing when people stopped engaging in these codependent behaviors. The people they loved were allowed to heal themselves, or in some instances, they never did heal, and the person was able to leave the relationship and find a self-love and peacefulness they would have never encountered had they not taken steps to change their behavior.

At this point in my life, it is easy to spot codependency, and I just want to grab the person at times and tell them, "Look, there is a better way that leads to true and lasting happiness," but then again, I have to check myself. I am here to share these lessons with those that ask for them. I can highlight how certain decisions related to similar experiences have allowed me to be free of guilt and pain, and then I can only pray for that person to be open to accept these suggestions. I am truly fortunate that God allowed Tami to become a part of my life to make me aware of these tools and to help me along the process of integrating them into my life. Without her love and her willingness to share her life lessons as they related to this and so many other things, would I have reached this point on my own? I am not sure. I do know that sharing these life experiences and learning opportunities with your spouse only helps to build and strengthen that relationship and helps to ensure a more open, honest, and healthy marriage.

In the end, I realize I am blessed to be in a marriage of equals. This is not to say that in each part of the marriage we have equal skill and contribute the same amount. Where I am deficient, Tami seems to excel. Where she struggles, I am blessed to be able to help out. In the end, we are equals because neither of us feels that we consistently contribute more to the marriage than the other. I certainly do not see a successful marriage as a fifty-fifty sharing of the load. At times, when I am struggling and working on my own issues, it seems as if Tami has to pull 90 percent of the load while the 10 percent I contribute is all I have left after working through my personal struggles. At times, that role flips, and I pull the weight of the relationship as Tami works on her issues. In the end, knowing that we have each other's back and knowing that at times we will have to bear the brunt of the responsibilities helps us to build an even stronger relationship. Knowing that God is always at the center binding us together is an incredible comfort as well. As we occasionally struggle and flow into and out of good places, God is a rock that we can tether ourselves to. As much as I try to always be a solid foundation, by my nature as a human, I am weaker sometimes than others. God is an unchanging fortress of strength that we can look to for support in our relationship when the other partner may be struggling as well.

CHAPTER 14
The Journey Continues

The more we allow God to take us over, the more truly ourselves we become.

—C. S. Lewis

Leaving the Corporate World

So here I was, nearing fifty years of time spent on this blue marble in the sky and had financially achieved more than I could have ever hoped for when I was young. Growing up in a trailer and using food stamps to buy our groceries, I had a dream as a child to simply get married and have a house when I was an adult. As I reflected on my situation as I neared the half century mark, I felt really blessed. I had healthy and productive children who seemed to be living a happy life. I had gotten remarried to Tami, a beautiful wife whom I was deeply in love with. I had a big house with an inground pool that overlooked a lake and had a forest of mature trees to greet me each morning when I awoke and looked out my window. I had made it indeed.

The problem was, I had no time to enjoy any of these many blessings in my life. As I had ascended the corporate ladder, I had taken a position in my company that had much more responsibility. While my pay was increased to match that responsibility, it required me to sell our home in Michigan and relocate to Missouri. With that relocation was the requirement to end my hospice care, my classes at the seminary, my blood donations, my volunteering at the soup kitchen, and all the things that fed my soul. In the end, after talking about it with my wife, we felt the additional pay would help us pay off some bills and help get us to a better place financially. I had also become a bit bored with my job in Michigan, as I am always apt to do, and this new challenge really interested me from a professional perspective. How would I handle being thrown into the crucible of factory life and dealing with UAW-represented hourly people? All my professional career, I had primarily managed salaried engineers and project managers, so this would be a good challenge for me.

This new job would also move my wife and I hundreds of miles away from our children. Though they were growing up and starting to take care of themselves, it would be difficult not to see them on a daily or even weekly basis. The two oldest boys had moved out and had their own places by this time. Our third son would eventually move to Missouri with us for a short time as he completed high school. Our youngest daughter had moved in with her father prior to us moving to Missouri, so she already had a safe place to stay. There was really nothing stopping us from making this move.

This move was a big move for both of us, but for my wife especially. Having never lived outside of Michigan and never being far from her support group, she felt this was indeed going to be a big step for her. Being a wonderful and genuine person, she would connect with others in the area we were moving to and make new friends. I did not anticipate that she would have to buoy up her support group because of my complete lack of presence at home once my job really started to exert the pull on me that I willingly let it. We were hundreds of miles away from home and family and my wife was basically on her own as I was at home for no more than an hour or two a day before falling asleep so I could rise early the next day and start the cycle again.

We had achieved what to many seemed like an ideal life. We had nice stuff, good friends, attended a nice church each weekend, and had a loving and strong relationship. What was not seen was the lack of a true center in our life. We were both working so hard that we had no time to enjoy all that we had worked so hard for. We had worked hard to build a loving and honest marriage, and we had little time to enjoy it. We were best friends but never had time to see each other. It was not unusual for me to arrive at work by 5:30 a.m. so I could try to catch up on e-mails before the meetings started at 6:30 a.m. I would bounce from meeting to meeting, from e-mail to e-mail, and by the time I looked up at night, it was 6:00 p.m., and I was still behind on everything I had to do. Not to say that I was not able to accomplish a lot during my time at this job, but the tasks were so big and so many, I could never really "catch up." I would arrive home by 6:30 p.m. or so, grab some dinner, and talk with Tami for a bit. Having been so busy at work all day in meetings and talking with people trying to solve issues, I really just wanted thirty to sixty minutes at home to read, relax, scroll social media, or something mindless to relax. The problem was, when I was done with this, I was ready for bed. Tami and I would try to watch a show on TV, and within ten minutes, I would be sleeping on the couch. When she tried to talk to me, I would listen but not really hear. I was already planning for the next day of work or trying to solve a problem from today. I was home, but not there. I was in a relationship but not present.

Looking down the road of my career, I realized it looked to be just more of the same. As I might get promotions, the demands on my time would increase and the requirement to begin traveling again would likely increase. As I looked at my bosses, I saw them even busier than me. Getting up in the middle of the night to use the restroom and checking their e-mails in the middle of the night. Struggling to take even one day off a week and spending that day writing business plans, agendas for the week, reflection on the prior week's performance. I saw no end in sight to the demands of my career and wondered if my marriage was destined again to fail because I had become a silent partner in the relationship.

I felt like I had started to lose control of my life a bit as I became more and more engaged in my work. The sad thing was, as usual, I didn't really seem to mind that problem most of the time. I was and am always so eager to please; the excitement of the job and the desire to be the best at it overcame my questions about balance when I was at work. When working, which was most of the time, I was all in and focused on the challenges in front of me and how to come up with new solutions to old problems. It was only when I had time to be present at home and really reflect on things that the questions arose.

My wife had also noticed, quite understandably, the issues. She had anticipated moving to a new state and going on adventures together, and more and more she was having to sort out things on her own. While she is perfectly capable of this, as a married team, there are many things you anticipate working on together. We had many talks about how in the world we would ever find a happy medium between work and life with this schedule and the demands of my career. We both realized that the schedule and pace we were running at was not sustainable and not what we had envisioned when we had gotten married just a few years earlier.

I believe it was my wife that first suggested the idea of a radical change. Perhaps going to a lower-paying job with less responsibilities to allow me more time at home. As we looked at the different opportunities, I came across a video on some social media platform about a couple that was in the same situation, and they had sold their belongings and bought a recreational vehicle, an RV, and took to the road. They shared pictures of their adventures traveling around the country, and the images were incredible. What a cool life, we both thought. But it was not possible for us. I still had spousal support payments from my first marriage for several more years, we had bills that were required, and we needed to take care of health insurance. So many hurdles that seemed insurmountable that this sort of lifestyle didn't seem realistic. But there was a small voice in my mind that was telling me to do this—find out what it would take and really look at this opportunity.

So, like all things that need a plan, I decided to really research the possibility of giving up all our material possessions, leaving my job, and hitting the road. I started out by making a list of all the financial requirements that I had to cover for the next few years, the bills that would still remain if we sold the house and got rid of our things. The number seemed like a reasonable amount so that in itself did not seem to be a roadblock. I would need some income, but perhaps I would be able to do some part-time contract work to cover the bills.

After making a number of spreadsheets with the bills we would have and the income I would have to work with from my bonus at work, the profits from selling out home and various other sources, my wife and I thought that, yes, this is a real possibility. We then researched many YouTube videos of "full timers." Full timers are folks who have done just that, live full time in an RV and travel the country. Some are constantly on the move while others find locations and stay for months or years at a time, but all share the same common denominator, they don't own a home, and they live, full time, in an RV.

The next big decision was to decide what type of RV we would want to live in as a home. We thought that maybe we should start inexpensively for our first foray into this adventure. Not knowing for sure if we would like being homeless and traveling the country like gypsies, maybe we should get a relatively inexpensive, preowned RV and see how it fit our lifestyle choice. We looked for what seemed like months on all sorts of RV trader websites, social media pages, and other spots. We researched the differences between class A, B, and C RVs, whether we should get a gas or diesel unit, how old of a unit should we consider, what brands had the highest customer satisfaction with the least number of issues. The options were almost endless, and in the end, we decided this was something we were going to pursue.

One of the next decisions was when I would tell my boss at work about my decision. I was officially going to retire. I was fifty-one at the time and had really worked my way into a well-paying career. All the work I had put in was to get me to this point of my career where I could start to make a lot of money and bank it as the kids were basically on their own at this point, and we had acquired much of everything we needed. These were going to be the golden years of my career where all the hard work was really going to pay off. There was still hard work ahead and a lot of hours, but the compensation would be substantial. Though we had pretty much decided we were going to purse this path at the start of the new year, we felt it would be best to wait until the end of the first quarter of the year to tell my boss. At the end of the first quarter is when the GM salary staff gets their bonus, and still being insecure about my performance and value at work, I was worried if I let my boss know well before that date, that it might affect my bonus, which we were counting on to help fund this little adventure. So, with those thoughts in mind, I decided to wait until March to share this decision with my boss.

I vividly recall telling my boss after our morning operations meeting that I wanted five or ten minutes with him when he had a chance that day. As we sat relatively close to each other in the front of the administration portion of facility, it was not uncommon for us to meet informally several times throughout the day. He knew that if I wanted a formal meeting, it was for something out of the ordinary. My boss at that time was a very talented and hardworking man. I learned a great deal from him and to this day have a lot of respect for him as a person and an employee. He truly was one of the hardest working individuals I had had the pleasure of working with. He expected a lot of himself and also a lot of those that worked for him. I appreciated his work ethic and his genuine care for those people that worked for him. At the facility we worked at, there were close to 4,500 employees, and he seemed to know most of them on a first-name basis. It was impressive to walk down the aisles of the factory and see so many people approach him and talk to him on a first-name basis.

As we walked into his office for our meeting, I closed the door behind us. This really caught his attention as usually this was reserved for just human relation or staffing type discussions that were highly confidential. I felt that little bit of nervousness well up inside me as I started the discussion. "Boss, you're probably not going to believe this, but I have decided to retire effective the end of May of this year." I kind of just blurted out to get it out on the table. At first, there was a bit of stunned silence on his part. He looked at me to see if I was joking or what the next line would be.

Finally, after what seemed like a very long silence, he said, "Retire, like retire, retire?"

"Yes," I said. I could tell he was taken completely off guard, which did not happen a lot to him.

"How could you retire now at this point in your career?" he asked several times. This is what I had been working toward. Would I be interested in staying on and transferring to a new location? Was it the job, was it him, was it something else that he could help with? He didn't really know how to respond, and neither did I; it was my first time retiring as well.

"Well, let me talk to Dan," he said. Dan was his boss. I think end of May will be fine. It was still eight weeks away, so I had left plenty of time for them to locate a replacement for me. Before we announced anything, he asked me to really think for a day or so before he called his boss to see if I would change my mind. I told him that I had been thinking about this for nearly six months and I was not going to change my mind at this point, but I would talk to my wife and let him know. After reconfirming later that week that this was in fact what I wanted to do, the process was put in place, and I started executing the details of the plan that my wife and I had put together.

We had found an RV that we were interested in but waited until we had gotten my bonus so we could put a substantial down payment on it. We decided to go with a class A diesel pusher. This is the type of RV that you sit in while you drive it. It is not the type that you tow behind your truck. They are big and look like a long box on wheels. They are called diesel pushers because they have a large diesel engine, usually the same size as a semitruck you can see hauling loads down the highway, located in the back of the unit that pushes the RV. We felt that we needed a diesel RV because our plan had developed such that we were looking to purchase an enclosed car hauler trailer that we would tow our SUV and motorcycle around behind the RV. So, the engine and tow capacity of the unit had to be such that it could handle the weight up and down the mountains we planned to traverse.

These class A RVs typically have slide outs in them that once you get parked in a location, they can extend out and increase the living space inside the unit. The

RV we found was a preowned model that had very high customer satisfaction with very few issues. The unit was a little over ten years old but looked almost brand new. It was owned by an older couple not more than an hour from our house. It really fit the criteria of what we were looking for. I joke with people that what really sold me on this RV was as I was scrolling through the online pictures of it, the owners had a picture of the front dash area. On the front dash, they had an 8.5×11 framed picture of Pope Francis. As a Catholic, there is no more tangible sign that this is the RV for you than when you see a picture of the vicar of Christ on the front dashboard.

Prior to telling my boss I was retiring, we had met with a real estate agent about selling our home. We had originally thought we would list it for sale by owner, and we had put a sign out in front of the house and didn't really have a lot of interest. A few people called, but the house didn't really seem to be generating the interest we had hoped for. When we met with Susan, the real estate agent, we explained our plan, and she said she would lower her commission by a few points because she was impressed with our plans to give our stuff away and pursue our dreams. We had worked with Susan when we bought the home just a few years earlier. We had hoped to sell our house on our own to keep the commission cost, but dealing with her made the process much easier, and we felt it was worth the money we would give up by using a licensed agent. Within three or four days of listing the house through Susan and her agency, we had an offer that was close to our asking price. We then realized, wow, this is really happening. It was at that point that all of the planning we had done and all the spreadsheets we had made with all the steps required really proved useful. There was some stress, for sure, but having a plan on paper in front of us allowed us to focus on the next step instead of worrying about all the things that could go wrong and how the timing would work on everything.

One of the first things we figured out is that in this country, you have to live somewhere even if you don't really live anywhere specifically. We were selling our home and hitting the road, but we needed a driver's license with an address from somewhere. We didn't own a home and planned to be traveling around the country, so what address would we have on our license? It was during this time that we learned about legal domiciles, mail forwarding companies, and all the things that are required for full time RV-ers. One of our relatives had a house in a state that was friendly toward RV full-time lifestyles. We visited this relative at least once a year, and she informed us that we could use her house as our domicile address. We did stay there as much as any one place throughout the year, so it seemed like a logical choice. After learning the licensing requirements of that state, we found they are very different state by state; we went there and completed all the required paperwork at the friendly local department of motor vehicles. Again, all the information was available online, and between that and calling that state's DMV, we had a pretty good idea of what was required. Prior to going there, we had taken all the steps of changing bank information, credit card information, and cell phone company to the new address. We were then able to take in these forms of proof of residency when we completed the paperwork.

The other thing we discovered is that the United States post office delivers almost anywhere, but they need to know where you are so they can deliver the mail. When one is picking up and moving to a new state each week, it makes it difficult for anyone to keep up with you. Thus, the invention of the mail forwarding services. Full-time RV-ers often utilize a mail forwarding service for this purpose. A mail forwarding service is a business that allows people to use their address as their mailing address. They collect all your mail and will forward to you at any location you tell them when you get settled for a bit. Nowadays with almost everything electronic, the amount of snail mail that is actually important or relevant continues to dwindle, but there are still occasions when paper checks are sent or cards from friends or loved ones arrive. This service proved to very valuable for us. Once we did hit the road, we would call every three weeks or so and have our mail sent to us at an RV park where we would be staying.

The single most time-consuming details I had to work out when we decided to execute this grand adventure was how to deal with the health care requirements. In the United States after the passing of the affordable care act, it was mandatory that we have some sort of insurance. Also, being on the road, and generally getting a bit older, the thought of having no health care and having a catastrophic health care event was worrisome for both of us. Unfortunately for me, I had hired into General Motors in 1998, and at this point, they had discontinued health care for retired salaried employees. It was assumed that most folks would work until they were near the age of Medicare and Medicaid and thus would not have to fund their own insurance. I had chosen however to retire fifteen years or so before I would be eligible for these services, so how was I going to fund my insurance? I could have extended my company-funded insurance through the COBRA alternative, but the price was highly prohibitive. It was basically a mortgage payment each month for insurance, and that was not something we had budgeted into our costs. After, again, a lot of research, I discovered the health share alternative. In this program, which is clearly stated as not insurance as they are not obligated by law to pay your claims, there is a group of people that send in a defined monthly contribution. The company, which is a nonprofit, accumulates these payments and sends out reimbursement checks to its members who have health care costs. The cost of this plan was about one-fifth the cost of the COBRA option and seemed like a good alternative. As both my wife and I were in good physical shape, this would cover us in the event of something terrible happening, and it also provided for wellness checkups and other small items. It really is a shame that living in one of the wealthiest nations in the world that the government has not found a way to reasonably fund health care for all of its citizens. It is a bit embarrassing to see so many other countries where this is offered, and everyone in those countries just takes it for granted as part of the government program in the country they live.

As the big day came to sell the house and get ready to vacate our home, we had to decide what to do with all the stuff we had accumulated. Often this process takes place when the parents get old and have to move into an assisted-living facility or dies and leaves a houseful of stuff. In my career as a hospice care volunteer, I had seen many family battles over stuff. Often, I think the value of these items is inconsequential; it just causes issues with the children as they argue about what's fair and who deserves what. We thought this would be a great opportunity to preemptively avoid this situation. We made a list, yet another spreadsheet, of everything we owned. We went through the house room by room, went through the basement, the garage, and the shed. We listed everything that we thought anyone would want and then identified what items we would be taking with us in the RV for our travels. Things we kept like laptops, clothes, a few books, and other personal items likely would not have been something our kids really wanted anyway. After that, we let the kids decide among themselves who would get what items. Fortunately for us, our two oldest sons were going to buy homes that year, and they would need all the stuff we were giving them to populate their new homes. Things like big screen TVs, new furniture, riding lawnmowers, beds, office furniture, all would be very helpful to first-time homeowners. It was a real sense of satisfaction for Tami and me to be helping our kids with their first homes in this way. I've never really figured out the dollar value of the items we gave away because it didn't really seem to matter. We just felt so happy it was going to our children. The idea of our kids fighting over our stuff as we got old was now a moot point as we no longer had anything for them to fight over. I was surprised how easily and smoothly the division of our stuff went between all the kids. Everyone selected what they wanted, and if there was something two kids wanted, they seemed to easily work through it and chose something else.

 When the time came to actually move out of the house, the kids drove to Missouri from Michigan and rented a big thirty-eight-foot moving truck. Over the course of two days, we loaded up all the stuff I had worked my life to accumulate and packed it into the back of a moving truck. We thought about where they would unload first and packed all that stuff in the back of the truck while all the stuff that went to other kids that would get unloaded last went into the front of the truck. It was two very long days loading up a huge truck, but after it was over, we could look around the house and see that there was very little stuff that we owned. There was however a whole garage full of items that they had left behind that they did not want for their new homes. What were we going to do with all these remaining items, we wondered. We decided anything we could not sell on Craigslist or Facebook, we would donate to the local Salvation Army or St. Vincent DePaul.

We listed a table online for sale for $20. It was likely worth far more, but we really just wanted to get rid of the stuff. A man named Carlos called and said he was interested and would be right over. He came and looked at the table and said for sure he wanted it. He was a nice guy and sounded like he had just come into the country from Mexico. He had a heavy accent and was very kind. He then asked us what we were going to do with everything else in the garage. We told him that if we didn't sell it, we would give it away. He then immediately asked if he could buy it all. Dumbfounded, my wife and I kind of looked at each other and said sure; he could take it all. He asked how much, and we told him he could just take it if he had a truck to move it. He was beyond grateful. It turns out that this whole family had just come to the area, and they had basically come into the country with only the clothes on their back and not much else. This would be a huge help in getting them started on a life here in the States. We felt very blessed knowing that the remaining stuff we had left would be going to someone who really needed it and that they would be moving everything themselves. We would not have to pack up things and take to the donation center. Five pickup trucks later, he had taken everything we had left that we did not want to take in our RV and that our kids did not want. Carlos was so grateful and so appreciative to us for all the items; it made us feel great that we were able to help him.

I remember to this day a special moment during the final part of our giving away of our possessions. As we had put some items out to the trash that we didn't think anyone would want, we saw Carlos and his friends pull two wooden swords out of the garbage we had put out front. These swords were old and maybe made by me or the kids as a school project. Carlos and friends were joking around and playfully sword fighting at the end of our driveway as we rode away on our motorcycle for a ride. The simple joy of playing with another while so much was going on in his life really reminded me of the importance of not taking things so seriously and allowing ourselves the time to laugh and have fun. Carlos, thanks for teaching me again the importance of laughter.

With my retirement papers signed, the house sold, the RV and trailer purchased and loaded with what items we decided to keep, it was time to finish up my last few weeks of work and begin this new adventure that we had chosen.

Hitting the Road

In the time between our planning to sell the home and retire and actually doing that, we had about six months of work before we could actually hit the road. During that time, we made a general, I should actually say very specific, plan of where we wanted to visit during our first year on the road. We decided we would travel up to Michigan first to visit our family and friends before embarking on this great journey. After spending a month or so there, we would head west and north through the upper part of the country before taking a sharp right turn at Montana and heading all the way up to Alaska for several months.

We both loved our Benedictine community as well as being outdoors, so our travels would focus on hitting the amazing national parks that the United States has as well as Benedictine monastic communities throughout the country. This way, we could see God's beauty in all of His creations, His people, and His natural outdoor beauty.

Always the planner, I had made a list of the national parks I wanted to visit as well as all the monasteries along the way. Being thorough, I listed the parks and monasteries in the order we would come upon them based upon our travel route. For driving purposes, I listed the addresses, websites, and the expected average temperatures when we were visiting. There is a thing in RVing called chasing the seventies. In this, you travel to locations and keep moving around so that the area you are in at that time will be around seventy degrees. This way, you don't need heat or air-conditioning, and the temperatures are just right. As you can see, the travel plans took into account the average temperatures, so we could indeed chase the seventies around the country. My detailed engineering and project management background has proven very useful for travel planning as well. My wife says that she simply just tells me certain things she might like to see in different areas of the country and then lets me handle all the planning. That makes her happy, and I get to feed my need for organization and planning. It is indeed a marriage made in heaven.

Area to visit	State	Address	Website	Month to visit	Average T	Nearest RV Park	RV Park Website	Park Address	Comments
Holly, MI	Michigan			1 - June 2018	79 High 57 Low	Covenant Hills RV Park	http://www.covenanthills.org/gly-camping	Covenant Hills Camp & Retreat 10359 E Fish and Rd, Otisville, MI 48463 P: 810-631-4531	E:	Starting point of Trip - Visit vet and family prior to departure - RV park is $17.50 per night thru Passport America
Duluth - Benedictine College	Minnesota	1001 Kenwood Avenue, Duluth, MN, 55811 218-723-6599	http://www.duluthbenedictines.org/monastery	1 - June 2018	71 High 45 Low	Indian Point Campground	http://duluthindianpoint.campground.reservations	7000 Pulaski St, Duluth, MN	$45 dollars per night for full hookup - Also do day trips to Voyageurs National Park north of Duluth
Assumption Abbey	North Dakota	418 3rd Avenue W, Richardton, ND	www.assumptionabbey.com	1 - June 2018	76 High 53 Low	North Park Campground	http://www.campnorthpark.com	701 227 8458 / 2330 Buckskin Drive / Dickinson, ND	1 hour drive from Theodore Roosevelt National Park
Theodore Roosevelt National Park	North Dakota	Medora, ND	https://www.nps.gov/thro/index.htm	1 - June 2018	76 High 50 Low	North Park Campground			Weekly - $207
Poor Clares of Montana	Montana	3020 18th Ave S, Great Falls, MT	www.poorclaresmt.org	1 - June 2018	73 High 46 Low	Not Required - Stay at Monastery	Not Required - Stay at Monastery		
Yellowstone National Park	Wyoming		https://www.nps.gov/yell/index.htm	2 - July 2018	72 High 40 Low	Valley View RV Park	http://valleyviewrvpark.us/sub2.com/	5152 N. Hwy 20, Island Park, Idaho	$60 per night or $550 per month - much cheaper on Passport America
Grand Tetons National park	Wyoming		https://www.nps.gov/grte/index.htm	2 - July 2018	62 High 42 Low				
Sawtooth wilderness Area	Idaho	Ketchum, Idaho	www.sawtoothsociety.org	2 - July 2018	81 High 45 Low	Smiley Creek Lodge & RV Park		18546 N Highway 75, Sawtooth City, ID 677.774.3547	$34 per night Full Service
Monastery of St. Gertrude	Idaho	465 Keuterville Rd, Cottonwood, ID	https://www.stgertrudes.org/	2 - July 2018	75 High 50 Low				
Glacier National Park	Montana		https://www.nps.gov/glac/index.htm	2 - July 2018	81 High 45 Low	Koocanusa Resort & Marina	http://www.koocanusaresort.net/rvtent-rsort/	Koocanusa Resort 23911 Scenic HWY 37 Libby MT 59923 Phone: 406-293-7474	$31.00 Per Night $175.00 Per Week $600.00 Monthly
Calgary, Alberta (Canada)	Alberta			3 - August 2018	78 High 50 Low				
Edmonton, Alberta (Canada)	Alberta			3 - August 2018	75 High 50 Low				
Dawson Creek (Canada)	Alberta			3 - August 2018	70 High 52 Low				
Denali National Park	Alaska	Denali, Alaska	https://www.nps.gov/dena/index.htm	3 - August 2018	66 High 46 Low	Trapper Creek	http://www.trappercreek.bl/lodging	PO Box 13209 Trapper Creek, AK 99683	Email is info@trappercreekinn.com

We did realize that we wanted our travel to have some structure but not be overly stringent. When I listed the timeframe we would be visiting each area, I generally just listed the month. We wanted the flexibility to stay a week or two or longer in certain areas if we really liked them and also to be able to get up and leave if the area was not what we liked or was not what we expected. Indeed, throughout our travels, we fell in love with certain areas and extended our stay. We may have bypassed certain other areas, but we figured we were still pretty young to be living this lifestyle, me in my early fifties and my wife in her midforties, so we would have plenty of time to come back and visit places we may not have seen on our first go around.

As we left Michigan and headed west, after traveling through the upper peninsula of Michigan, we made our first extended stop in Duluth, Minnesota. A beautiful city on the banks of Lake Superior, it is a wonderful place to visit and a great place to live, if you don't mind brutally cold winters. We do, so we decided to just visit in the summer. We had visited Duluth a year or so earlier for a Benedictine conference at St. Scholastica college and monastery and fell in love with the community. So, prior to hitting the road, we had e-mailed one of the sisters at the monastery to see if we could park our RV in the huge lot they have for students, who would be gone for the summer, and hang out in Duluth for a week or two and attend daily prayers with the sisters at St. Scholastica. With typical Benedictine hospitality, Sr. Edith replied that of course we could stay, and she looked forward to seeing us. As it was throughout our journeys, we were blown away with how kind and caring most everyone we met along the way treated us. In the news, we see so many stories of angry people and political unrest and division. When we traveled, we met wonderful, loving, and kind people who were happy to show us their community and share their stories. God had blessed us richly indeed with safe travels and kind people.

Leaving Minnesota, we continued to travel west to where the United States takes on beauty that seems almost unreal in its grandeur. Being a simple writer, I have an inadequate vocabulary to even being to describe the beauty that God painted with his eternal paintbrush across the western landscapes. Being from the Midwest, seeing majestic snow-capped mountains rising out of the plains in the distance was something I was not prepared for. No matter how many times you might see them on TV shows and magazines, experiencing the soaring majesty of the Rocky Mountains as they create a sawtooth profile that rips apart the horizon is not something you can see and not be moved by. It is breathtaking in its beauty and alarming in its reality to consider I would be driving my RV and trailer up and down those magnificent slopes.

On our way west, we had planned to visit Assumption Abbey in Richardton, North Dakota. Built around 1906, the abbey towers above the cornfields in the area. The twin steeples rise above the horizon like pinnacles of history, reaching up toward heaven. As we entered the town of Richardton off the highway, not really sure exactly which way to go, we just spied the spires off in the distance and followed the road leading to these beautiful towers. Pulling into the ample parking lot on a cool midweek afternoon, we had no problem finding space to park our RV. Built when Catholic religious life and parish attendance was booming, the parking lots of many monasteries and abbeys can easily hold hundreds of cars. Now as the number of monastic vocations and mass attendance has dwindled, its typically easy to find a parking spot even if the vehicle you're driving is as large as a tractor trailer.

As we parked the rig, leveled her up, and extended the slides, it was not more than a few minutes than our host, Brother Louie, exited the monastery and greeted us. Exceedingly kind and generous, Brother Louie immediately made us feel like we were home with his gracious attitude and loving demeanor. The monastery was built, as most are, on the top of a hill overlooking the surrounding area. The views from the hill were breathtaking, and the quietness and peacefulness were apparent as soon as we settled in.

Sharing a meal and prayers with the community was a wonderful experience. During prayers, instead of having us sit out in the pews, the monastic community of monks invited us up into the area where the monks say their prayers. Many of the monks went out of their way to greet us and welcome us. Throughout our journey, I was amazed and the kindness of so many people. No one exemplified this kindness more than the monks and other religious we met during our travels. As the brothers took their afternoon strolls outside, many stopped by the RV to check out this motorized behemoth that had taken up temporary residence in their parking lot. Many had never been inside an RV, and they found the concept of a house on wheels very interesting. Since we have many religious icons in our RV, some commented that it felt like a rolling chapel. I liked that description very much.

I took a picture during our stay there that to this day stands out in my memory as one of my favorites. In the lower left corner of the picture, our RV is parked. It seems so small in this picture, dwarfed in size by the immense towers of the abbey on the right side of the pictures. It appears to me that the RV is kneeling at the foot of the cross, paying homage to the beauty that is before it. To me, this picture encapsulates the vastness of God when compared to our human plight. Each day we struggle with things that may seem like life and death, or at least so critical, we focus all our attention on them. God, meanwhile, has had prayers directed at Him throughout the millennia, all claiming to be urgent, life-shattering, the most important. In reality, our individual needs and desires are so small in the scope of the vastness of God's creation and His love. To me, the little RV in the corner, which seems so big to me when I stand next to it, represents me and my human plight while the abbey represents God and his majesty and incomprehensible vastness. Some may see it as just another travel picture, but for me, it summarizes the relationship between man and God. All these thoughts captured from the lens of my iPhone.

As we entered into Montana and explored Glacier National Park, the Grand Tetons (or Grand Croutons as my boys nicknamed them when we did our out west adventure some fifteen years earlier) and Yellowstone, we were so happy we had decided to include our Harley Davidson motorcycle along with our SUV in the trailer we were towing. To be able to setup in an RV park and pull out the Harley to be able to ride through the national parks opened up the adventure to us in a way that is indescribable if you have never ridden a motorcycle. Instead of visually seeing the sights through a car's small window in front and to the side of you, you see the entire landscape with no filter and no restricted vision. Everywhere you turn, there is only natural beauty and no restriction to what you can see. In addition to seeing the beauty of the creation all around you, you can feel it. You can taste the sweetness of the air as you ride through a flowering meadow. You can smell the trees in bloom and, sometimes unfortunately, the smell of roadkill and every scent that natural creation has to offer. When you drive through a national park in a car, you see its beauty. When you drive through a national park on a motorcycle, you become part of that park and experience stimulation to all of your senses. You can get into small spaces that being in a car or RV does not allow.

As we drove through Glacier National Park, we were blessed that the famed Going to the Sun Road had been opened to through traffic. This is typically not open until June or July as it takes that long to clear all the winter snows from the road. We were able to take that drive on our motorcycle, and it was an experience that I shall never forget. Like most national parks in the lower 48 in the summer, there was traffic to contend with. When it got to be a little too much, all I needed was a few open feet of space, and I could easily pull my motorcycle off to the side of the road and just take a break and look at all of God's beauty as it surrounded and enveloped me.

Primed for what lay ahead after experiencing Glacier and Yellowstone, we decided to head to the great white north. The land of enchantment and adventure, the last great frontier of the United States, Alaska. I had dreamed of visiting Alaska since my youth when I saw pictures from my grandfather as he traveled there in an RV with my grandmother and my uncle when I was in elementary school. Since then, I had read and watched just about everything I could about this vast landscape. It seemed almost unreal in size and beauty. And now, here I was about to begin my journey to my dream location.

We turned north after visiting Glacier National Park and attempted to cross into Canada at the Sweetgrass border entry location in Montana. We anticipated that it might be a bit of an adventure trying to get into Canada. We had our dog George with us who was partially pit bull, but we had all the required papers and canine vaccination records. We also had a shotgun in our RV for personal protection, but we had the paperwork for that completed as well. After sharing all this with the Canadian customs official at the entry point, he asked us to pull over into the inspection area and come on in. Not surprising, but we had hoped we would be able to get through with just a few questions. As we entered and approached the desk, the officer waved us over to his area. To our surprise, there was a substantial issue with Tami's passport and the required paperwork. He looked at it for a bit and advised that while I would be able to proceed, Tami's paperwork was not in order, and she would not be allowed to enter Canada at this time. We were both kind of dumbfounded. We thought he must have made a mistake or there was a mix-up. All of our plans had us going to Alaska for several months and in no plans were there options for either of us to go on our own. We slowly walked out of the office, completely unsure of what to do next. We decided to do what we do best when we needed to figure something out—talk about it over a meal. We drove back to Shelby, Montana, where we had started the day from with our RV and trailer in tow behind us. We figured this was a difficult decision relative to what our next steps would be, so we decided on Mexican food for lunch.

We had to decide how to proceed. We had maps and plans and agendas, but not being able to head north was a major impact to what we thought we were going to do. After slowly working through the free chips and salsa, we decided on a couple of options. Either scrap the whole Alaskan adventure idea and just head west to Washington state and work our way down the coast, or I would drive alone across the Alaskan Highway, and Tami would stay in Montana and fly up there once I reached the forty-ninth state. It was a tough choice either way. Scraping the plans to head to Alaska was something I really didn't want to do. I had wanted to go for the last forty years of my life only to be turned away so close. Traveling separate was not what we had in mind, and there was the added costs of flights and hotel stays. After pondering our options over a burrito smothered in cheese sauce with a side of beans and rice, we decided that we were going to get to Alaska one way or another. I cannot say that the thought of trying to sneak Tami into Canada in our RV did not cross my mind, but I thought they would for sure thoroughly search the rig when I came back to the border checkpoint. So, we found a hotel in Great Falls where Tami would stay for a week until I made it through Canada and arrived in Fairbanks. We called and checked on the price of airline tickets and hotels. It would not be cheap, but what was the cash value of visiting a place you had always dreamed about?

Being partners in life and in this adventure, it was really hard saying good-bye in Great Falls after Tami had checked into the hotel. For me, I have found that the joy in adventure when traveling to new spots is enhanced when you have someone to share it with. I was going to travel several thousand miles through Canada through the Rockies and through breathtaking beauty but have no one to share it with except George, our family dog and trusty traveling companion. There were a few tears shed as I slowly rolled the rig out of the hotel parking lot and waived to Tami as she slowly faded away in my rearview mirror.

The trip through Canada was nothing short of spectacular in its grandeur in beauty. Driving through the snow-capped mountains, even though it was June, and stopping alongside fast-moving streams that were ice-cold due to the snow runoff was something I'll always recall. I saw bears, mountain goats, bison, and every kind of wildlife the country had to offer. It really felt like I was leaving the city and tamed environment of the lower 48 and entering into a time when nature was free and wildlife was abundant. I was so thankful to God for this experience, but sad that my best friend was not there with me.

As much as I loved the scenery, I hurriedly made my way along the 2,200-mile trip from Sweet Grass, Montana, to Fairbanks, Alaska, where I would reunite with my love. Instead of pulling over and staying for days at some remote yet breathtakingly beautiful sight, I might pull over for a sandwich and a few pictures but would keep on moving so as to meet my wife again and start our shared adventure again. If you have never driven the Alaskan Highway from the lower 48 to Alaska at least once in your life, it should be something you add to your list of things to do. I don't like the term bucket list as it seems overused and cliché. When I was in my early twenties, a colleague from work told me about an idea to make a list of fifty things you wanted to do or visit or achieve in your life. I had never thought about it until then, but I sat down then and made my top fifty list.

Visiting Alaska was near the top of that list and one of the few things I had not crossed off my list.

As I made my way across the Canadian landscape, I realize how vast a wilderness area this still was. I might drive for an hour or so and maybe see only one other car and no towns or gas stations. Lucky for me, the RV has a one-hundred-gallon gas tank, so even though I only get about 7.5 miles per gallon, I can go a very long way between fill-ups. This was fortunate because there were times driving through the Canadian Rockies where it might be two hundred miles between service stations.

I found this vastness and distance between service stations to be painfully true as I pulled over one afternoon in the Yukon territory to use the restroom and take George for a walk. As I walked around the rig to do a visual inspection, I noticed a substantial amount of antifreeze on the back of the unit and a puddle forming under the RV. I opened up the rear vents and looked at the radiator and saw antifreeze everywhere. I am no certified auto mechanic, but I was able to quickly deduce that this was not good. I got back into the RV and started to travel on, hoping it would make it to the next service station where I could look at it a bit more.

As I traveled down the deserted highway, my fears became reality as slowly the temperature gauge started to climb, and eventually, a warning light came on. I pulled over and added some water to the overflow tank, hoping that this addition of water would hold me over until I reached civilization. No luck, a few miles down the road, the gauge started to climb again. Not sure what to do, I pulled over and looked at the radiator again. It appeared that there was a leak somewhere, but I could not locate it. Some Canadian Mounties drove by in their car and asked if everything was okay, and not really knowing what they could do to help, I just shook my head yes. I knew the next town in front of me was in Alaska and several hundred miles ahead. I decided to turn back to the last town I had driven through which was Haines Junction, Yukon Territory. Of course, not every small town has a service center open to work on big diesel pusher RVs. And the fact that it was the weekend made it nearly impossible to even find anything open. I found a shop that was closed, but there was a person working on the inside. I asked him if anyone in town worked on RVs. "Nope, you'll either need to go a hundred miles back to Whitehorse or a few hundred miles ahead to Fairbanks," he said slowly as he looked at my RV.

Well, that was not the news I wanted to hear. I didn't want to go in the wrong direction for a hundred plus miles as I was supposed to meet Tami at the Fairbanks airport in a day or so. I decided I would take the advice of Boniface Wimmer and go "forward, always forward, everywhere forward." Since Abbot Boniface had arrived in the United States in the mid-1800s and helped form Saint Vincent Abbey in Latrobe, Pennsylvania, it seems likely he never owned an RV when he uttered this famous phrase of his.

So, forward I went. Every twenty or thirty minutes, the temperature gauge would rise, and I would have to pull over, let the rig cool down, and then add more water. I knew I could make it to Alaska as the rig has an eighty gallon freshwater tank, and I had plenty of water to draw from, but it would take me many days of travel if I kept having to stop and start. There was no way I would make it to the airport in Fairbanks in time, and Tami would be left waiting as I had no cell phone service and no way to let her know what was going on.

As I started driving again after adding more water, I grabbed my rosary and decided I would pray and ask for God's help with this. I know He has much bigger issues to resolve than allowing me to get to the airport on time, but I also know He is a loving father who gives His children what they need. Not necessarily what we want, but what we need. As I was praying, I decided that the next time I had to add water, I was going to empty my container of holy water into the radiator. Yes, I do travel with a container of holy water. You never know when you will need to exorcise a demon, fight a vampire, or ask for divine assistance with a radiator leak. So, thirty minutes later when I pulled over, I put the holy water into the tank. I saved a tablespoon full in case I ran across any vampires in this remote area of the Yukon. As I put it in the unit, I remember praying, "God, I know you are busy, but I know you have the power to perform miracles, and I would really appreciate any help you might want to give me on this." I started down the road again with a radiator circulating holy water through its punctured veins. I noticed after thirty minutes, the temperature gauge was holding steady. Then an hour and then two, and no change. I really might make it to Fairbanks, I thought. This is like a miracle here, I thought. Several hundred miles later, I pulled into the campground in Fairbanks, Riverview RV Park, and parked the rig next to the registration house. I had arrived late, and no one was there, but I had made it to Fairbanks. I opened up the slides on the RV and, after walking George and feeding both of us, crawled into bed, eternally grateful for God's help in getting me to my destination. After I had picked up Tami and made a few phone calls, I located a Cummins diesel repair shop in town. They let us park the rig in the parking lot while they checked it out. They pulled the radiator out of the unit and showed me the front face of it. It looked like it had been shot by a shotgun, with indentations from the stones all over the veins of the unit. "How in the world did you get this rig here?" they asked. "I imagine you must have had to add water every few minutes to keep it cool," they continued.

"Yeah, it was a miracle I made it here," I said to them, not sure they realized the accuracy of that statement. We ended up camping in the back of the Cummins parking lot for two weeks as they had to have a radiator specially made and flown in from the lower 48. Yes, it was as expensive as it sounds like it would be for that. But this time gave us the opportunity to spend some extra time in Fairbanks and explore the area, drive the Dalton Highway north, past the Arctic Circle, and slow down and rest. I've discovered that if we are open to it and see these times of stress as opportunities for growth and reflection, we can find beauty in most any situation. At the time what seemed like a major inconvenience and a costly issue led to some of the nicest times during our Alaskan adventure.

There are so many iconic locations on the way from the lower 48 to Alaska. There are beautiful mountains and hiking and camping areas. I had purchased old school paper maps as I knew cell phone service would be sketchy at best for many miles of the journey, and I loved reading maps and discovering new locations. In an age when you can Google anything and get pictures and reviews, I love pulling out a map and looking at names of towns and parks and trying to imagine them based upon their names, locations, and topography. I love having access to the information that technology allows for, but I love the mystery of times past when you didn't really know what to expect when pulling into some new remote location.

Finally arriving in Alaska after six days of hard driving, and a few mechanical issues, I was overjoyed to see the "Welcome to Alaska" sign near the border. Once I had cleared customs, it took no more than four or five minutes coming back into the United States from Canada, I had to pinch myself that I was actually in Alaska. All my years of dreaming of this had finally come true. I recall saying out loud to George, "We made it, buddy. We are here," and pumping my fist in the air. The joy was tempered a bit as I had to slow the rig down to about twenty miles per hour to avoid dishes flying everywhere as I flew across one frost heave to another. Due to the extreme cold they experience, Alaskan roads are subject to an unpleasant phenomenon known as frost heaves. The roads buckle due to the drastic change of climate, and it creates a whoop-de-do effect of one- or two-foot-high rises in the concrete every twenty or thirty feet along the road. While this would be great fun with a BMX bike or motocross motorcycle, it was far less enjoyable in a forty-foot-long RV that was towing a twenty-four-foot trailer. Regardless of how hard the trailer bumped up and down, I still could not wipe the grin off my face. I was in Alaska!

We ended up spending about two and a half months in the forty-ninth state. It was not nearly long enough to really explore all the beauty the state has to offer. We visited so many wonderful places and did so many hikes through beautiful parks and mountains; we really fell in love with the state. But so as not to turn this book into a travel diary (I am sensing an idea for my next book), we'll say that we moved on as the weather started to turn colder. It was nearing the end of August, and there were nights when we were starting to see the low forties. As we are dedicated seventy chasers, it was time to head south.

Again, not being able to travel through Canada, Tami flew ahead and waited for me to arrive in the lower 48. This time, with adequate time to plan, we had arranged for her to stay at a convent with the Poor Clares of Montana. This group of religious sisters was located in Great Falls and welcomed Tami to stay with them while I was traveling back through the Canadian Rockies. The Poor Clares of Montana website pretty clearly describes them and their goal,

> We, the Poor Clares of Montana, daughters of St. Clare and St. Francis of Assisi, are called to live the Holy Gospel in the contemporary Church. We are dedicated to a life of contemplative prayer in an enclosed community, dependent on God's providence, providing a place where all are welcome to experience God's presence and peace.

A small cloistered community, they were very kind to Tami for the week she stayed there, and upon arriving, I joined them for prayers, and I saw why Tami felt they were such a lovely group.

Traveling back to the lower 48 from Alaska, I had decided to take an alternate route from the trip north. Going north, we had been a bit shaken up by the discovery that Tami would not be able to make the drive. I was in a hurry to get to Fairbanks to meet here and took the most direct route I could map out. Coming back south, we had adequate time to plan for this, and knowing she would be in community with the sisters in Great Falls, I decided to visit Banff and Jasper and take a bit of a longer route home. Though it made the trip a few days longer, the views it afforded were spectacular. I was very sad that the only way Tami could see these sights was through the lens of my camera on my phone, but I appreciated the beauty God had put in front of me.

Reunited in Great Falls, we headed west again to visit Oregon and a friend we had made while at the Jain retreat center in Texas. Jamie is a wonderful young lady who lived near Bend, Oregon, and we had told her the previous year that we would likely be heading out west as part of our adventure. She, without hesitation, invited us to stop by her house and meet her family.

One of the amazing things I have experienced as I have changed my life from focusing less on work and material things and more on relationships, experiences, and love is the amazing, wise, kind, and loving people God has put in my life. Perhaps they have always been there, and only now am I taking time to appreciate them for who they are and not what they can give me or how they can help my career. It may also help that the majority of the people I interact with now are at retreats, on nature hikes, in church, or some sort of service work to others. Their lives are full of love, and that love cannot help but spill over into my heart as well. Like an athlete who always trains with someone who is more skilled than them to help improve their game, my caring and honesty tools have been improved by spending time with those far more loving, caring, and intelligent than me.

When we arrived in Oregon, we were amazed at the beauty of the coastline, of Crater Lake, and all the other natural beauty there. The radiance of Jamie's smile and the pride in her heart as she met us and introduced us to her young son were dazzling in their brightness. It is wonderful traveling the country on your own terms and own time schedule, and it is made even more spectacular when you meet amazing and loving people along the way.

Continuing on from Oregon, we headed south into California. One cannot travel through Northern California with stopping to stand in jaw-dropping awe of the size and majesty of the California Redwoods. To see these towers of nature thrust themselves hundreds of feet into the air, to stand at their base in awe of the sheer size of them is indeed humbling. To see the seeds that they grew from and realize such majestic wooden sentinels started from a seed that would fit in the palm of one's hand made me pause in the wonders of God's creation. If such spectacular natural wonders can arise from such a small seed, what do we have the potential to become if we turn our lives over to God in trust? These trees simply just exist. They do not strive for importance or seek rewards; they start as the humblest of seeds and just allow God to work on them over the centuries. God provides them all the nourishment they need to grow, and as long as man does not destroy them, they grow to spectacular heights. What if we as people just allowed God to nourish us and trust that He would provide, what would we grow into over time, if our fellow man did not destroy us? It is an excellent question to ponder.

When we were in California, we had planned to visit a special RV park that was part of the RV club we belonged to. It was near Yosemite, a national park that neither of us had ever visited before. Prior to arriving at the park, I had been contacted by a friend who had taken a job at a start-up electric car company in the San Francisco Bay Area, and he had asked me if I was interested in joining the team. I was a little intrigued as building a new plant and being on the ground floor of the planning was always the most enjoyable part of the job for me. I interviewed with the company, and they offered me a position. I had put myself back in the game if I chose to be and now had to decide what I wanted to do. I had left a corporate career for the freedom to travel, volunteer, and just work when I wanted. This would be a "real" job again. At least six days a week and a lot of hours. It would interesting, but at what cost? The real draw was the plant was being built in a part of the country we loved, so perhaps it made sense for us to abandon our plans of travel and volunteering and take the new job and the money it offered. "I'll have to pray about this for a bit," I told my friend Mike when he called me with the offer.

I attended a Sunday mass at a Catholic church in the Fresno area a few days after the offer came in. I went into the church thinking that

I really needed to pray about this and try to decide what direction I should take. I was strongly leaning toward taking this new challenge and entering the workforce again. I kneeled down in prayer, and it really took less than a few minutes for it to hit me like a thunderbolt. "You say you trust in my providence, Marty, yet you are hedging your bets to take the money now and give up on all that I have promised for you. Trust Me, and I will provide," the voice in my head boomed. It was such a powerful message; I told my wife immediately that I would not be taking the job after all and asked her if she supported this. My wife has always been the wiser partner in this relationship, and she saw quickly that this message had been given me, and she too trusted in what God had in store for us.

I called my friend back the next day and thanked him very much for the offer but told him at this time I would have to decline it. I didn't get into the details, but I truly felt that God had much better things in store for me if I just trusted. When I retired from GM at the age of fifty-one, I knew that I did not have enough money in my savings to cover me for the rest of my life. I had a good bit, and we were living modestly, but realistically, I expected to live another thirty to forty years, and I did not have that amount of scratch stored up in my savings. I was tempted to take the money that was in front of me with the job offer. What if I couldn't find a job when I was ready to work for a few months? But instead I heard a voice that if I only trusted, I would be taken care of financially and that I would be surrounded by love.

As we arrived at the RV park near Yosemite, we had gotten tired of traveling at the pace we had been. We had originally started by driving and staying a night or so then hitting the road again. We then slowed down a bit and would try to stay for a week or so before packing up and moving again. We still felt, even at that pace, that we were always packing and unpacking and not really allowing ourselves enough time to enjoy, and just be, to allow ourselves to be present and sit still like a Redwood while God worked on us. So, we decided we would stay in each location a bit longer to really feel the nature in the area and really meet the people who were our neighbors. When we arrived at the park near Yosemite, we had booked it for a week.

We fell in love with the park and extended our stay for another week. At the start of that week, we extended for yet another week after that. We had found a park that had a very homelike feeling. Many of the residents were long-term residents who owned their sites and met each day for coffee and community. The park had a woodshop so I could make things, and it was within forty-five minutes of El Cap in Yosemite National Park. We were smitten with what we had found.

After three weeks, we were hesitantly ready to move on. We looked at possibly making this our winter home when were old enough. It was a retiree's park that required its members to be fifty-five years old, so for the first time in many, many years, I was too young for something. Knowing that fall was coming, we pointed our rig south yet again and headed out for, literally, greener pastures.

Heading southeast from Yosemite, we were headed to one of our favorite places in the United States. Sedona, Arizona, is a mystical place to us. We have visited several times and each time find new adventures, new trails to hike, and the energy vortexes and the attitude of the people who live there is both powerful and soothing. When entering into the Red Rock Canyons that surround Sedona for the first time, you almost feel as if you are leaving the earthly terrain you are familiar with and entering a Martian landscape. Jutting cliffs of red rocks look like a picture that could have been beamed by the Martian rovers. I always have to pull over as I enter the area and just stop and take in the beauty of it all.

Once in Sedona, we hunkered down again for a few weeks. There is so much to see and do, and one of our favorite places to visit is Jerome, Arizona. As unique an old west town if ever there were one, it is now inhabited by a group of free-spirited folks who like to live a bit on the fringe. The views from the town are spectacular, and the vibe there is unique to any other place we have been.

From Arizona, it was on to our final travel destination for that year, the great state of Texas. We had been on the road for about eight months and had fallen in love with the full-time RV lifestyle; we had traveled north to Alaska, west to the shores of the pacific, and now south to the last bit of America before entering into Mexico. We had seen the Great American west from the windows of our RV. We had met too many amazing people to count and were immersed in love and gratitude. Nearly every morning we awoke with the sounds and smells of God's creation permeating our residence, and we were overcome with gratitude. "Can you believe we are living this life?" my wife and I asked of each other. We had given away nearly all that we owned, had left the security of a good-paying job for a future that was not guaranteed, and no longer owned a home. We were by many standards highly unsuccessful, and yet we had never been happier. Free of the encumberments of material possessions, we could just enjoy what God provided for us each day. A beautiful sunrise, an encounter with a moose, a tasty local meal, a good conversation with a like-minded individual: we were experiencing all of these things each day and were unbelievably grateful. Humbled by the generosity of a Father who was indeed so good. You can never outdo God in generosity, I had been taught in the seminary, and now I was seeing this come to full fruition.

Almost on cue, as I had turned down the full-time job I had been offered, I was offered a part-time short-term job assignment in Texas where I had hoped to spend the winter. After calculating what we thought we would need to live on for the upcoming year and how many months I would have to work, I started my new assignment with renewed vigor and an appreciation for my journey and what I had been able to experience that year.

Going Back to Work

Though I had only been "retired" for seven months, it seemed like so much had happened in that span of time. Having seven months off with no work for the first time in my life, I had found out what freedom looked like. Starting to work full time when I was fifteen, I had not had more than a few weeks off in a row for the last thirty-five years of my life. To be suddenly free of having to wake up at a certain time each and every morning was completely liberating and, truth be told, a bit disorienting as well.

I had kept in touch with many of my colleagues from work. When you spend nearly twenty years with a company and do the kind of highly challenging and stressful work I had done, you truly form lifelong bonds with many of your coworkers. As I first started my career at General Motors, being a road warrior, I would spend weeks and months out of town with coworkers. We would work long hours together and then often join each other for dinner as well. Then, as I transitioned to working in a single assembly plant, I really experienced the "team" aspect as we all struggled to achieve a common, quantifiable goal. These shared struggles built tremendous friendships with highly talented, humorous, and caring people.

When I retired, most of my colleagues were amazed that I had decided to step away at a relatively young age. What at first seemed like such hard work, having children at a young age, had really turned into a blessing as I had aged. I was able to step away from a corporate career at a young age because I did not have children at home that needed my income to support them. Many of my coworkers who were near my age had gone to college out of high school and waited a bit to start families so they did not have the freedom I did to walk away from their job so easily.

As I left my career and started on the grand adventure of touring the country in my RV, through the advent of social media, I was able to stay in pretty close contact with lots of my family and friends, many of which were coworkers. This connection with work colleagues allowed me to stay somewhat up to date with which projects were going on and when and where there would be help needed.

In the automotive industry in which I worked, production is king. The assembly plants run full out until there is a small break in time, usually no more than a week or two where they shut the plants down and retool the equipment to make new models or to allow the machinery to continue to run smoothly. These breaks in time, downtimes they are referred to, are typically hellish adventures of stress and tension. Millions of dollars of work are jammed into small, little windows of time, and God help you if the equipment is not ready to start back up when the downtime is scheduled to end. The downtimes, these times of intense stress, forge friendships that last longer than the equipment that was installed.

As I reflect back on my career, twenty years with General Motors and fifteen years as a supplier, I recall most of these downtimes very vividly. I cannot recall exactly what the scope of work was or what equipment we were replacing, but I can recall in great detail the struggles I went through and who was there with me to overcome the challenges. I will not compare these high-stress downtimes to war, because the end results of these are very different. At work, if we failed, we might get yelled at, have our pay affected, or even get fired, but in war if you fail, they may ship your body back to your family in a green bag. There were always comments like this in these downtimes. As the downtimes came to an end and work was far behind and it appeared we might not get done, someone would always ask who was shipping in the body bags and how many we needed. People would leave newspaper classified ads with job openings on someone's desk whose job wasn't going well, but it truly was never life and death, though it sure felt like it at times.

Invariably, when we would get through a downtime and the equipment would start up on time and we would make it, sometimes by mere hours or even minutes, everyone would shake their head and ask, "How did we do that?" When we would get together with our wives for a dinner, I would always wonder how the wives could stand these events as all us guys did was talk about our "war stories" as we called them. As our spouses had not been in the trenches, so many war analogies we used, they couldn't truly understand what we were talking about. They had to deal with us when we came home tired, frustrated, dirty, and wanting to just crash on the bed and be left alone.

When I had reached out to some of my friends at General Motors, after I had retired, suggesting I would be open to coming back as a contract engineer to help with the downtimes, I was surprised to see that there seemed to be a lot of interest. The field I had spent most of my career in was pretty specific, and there were not a lot of people who wanted to or had the skillset to work on these downtimes. I look around the jobsites and see there are not a lot of young kids getting into the industry. When I look at the job requirements, it is not hard to see why. You want me to travel all the time, work in a sometimes very hostile environment with high tension, mediocre pay, and little support?

Hey, buddy, it's not just a job. It's an adventure!

Sounds great. Where do I sign up?

Thankfully for me, this had been my life for many years, and I knew how to do this work well, and there continued to be a need for this type of support. I had reached out to my friends about possibly working at a certain plant during a certain time and was blessed to be able to join the team again as a contractor.

As we rolled into Texas with our RV, I felt a little like I was coming home. I had spent a lot of time at this particular GM plant over the years and had established good relationships with many of the people who worked there. Being a three-shift assembly with around four thousand people, there were always lots of new faces, but I thought it would be nice to walk back into work already knowing many of the people I would be spending the next few months.

When I had looked at our projected bills for the upcoming year, it looked like I would need to work three or four months to cover our costs until the following year. Not a bad deal, I thought, work four months and then take the next ten off. This was the kind of work-life balance I had been striving for ever since I entered the workforce as a young, hungry teenager.

Prior to arriving in Texas, we had found a nice RV park that was somewhat close to the plant. The RV park was a little expensive, but we figured we would be living there for the next four months, so why not splurge a little and have a nice park in a nice part of town, near Grapevine, Texas, to live in. As we were driving there, we started to think about the costs and the drive and wondered if we might find something better. Also, our plans had changed by a few weeks, and we would be arriving a few days earlier than we had originally made our reservations for. I called the park, and they did not have space to take us any earlier day than our original reservation allowed for. So, looking around, we found another park that I knew several of my friends would be staying at as well. I called and made reservations for the two weeks earlier we would be arriving and also reserved for the full four months. I figured why not have options. We'll check out this park, and if we don't like it, we'll move to the original park we had reserved and cancel the rest of our reservation at park number 2. As the check-in date came closer and as we were heading to Texas, traveling through New Mexico, we received an e-mail from the original park we had reserved. Due to flooding, the park would be closed for the next four to five months and our deposit would be returned. Due to the limited number of RV parks in the area, all other parks filled up immediately. If we had not had the second reservation, I am not sure where we have ended up staying. We felt very fortunate to have double booked and have had a nice place to stay during our visit.

As we were arriving a few days before I was to start, it allowed us to get settled and nestled in prior to me starting my work assignment. I had spent a lot of time in the area, but Tami had not, so I took the opportunity to play tour guide and show her the great state of Texas. Getting her comfortable and situated was important for me prior to starting work. I wanted to know that we were in a good and comfortable location because I knew the upcoming months would be very busy.

Arriving at work on my first day back, I was waiting in the lobby for my host to pick me up and take me back to my office. The first day or so always involves getting security badges, laptops, and all the other necessities. As I was waiting in the lobby, I couldn't believe my eyes as an old friend I had worked with over the last twenty years slowly walked into the lobby as well. "Larry, what are you doing here?" I asked him incredulously. His eyes lit up when he saw me.

"Marty, it's great to see you. Thank you so much! I am here because of you!" Puzzled, I was not really sure what he was talking about. He reminded me that just prior to me retiring, I had sent some e-mails over to the plant team here letting them know Larry was interested in coming to work here, and I was highly recommending him for a certain job. The notes had caught the attention of the right person, and they had in fact offered Larry a job transfer to relocate to Texas and potentially finish his career here, where he wanted to be. I was so very happy that I had been able to help him and remembered the most enjoyable part of my job prior to retiring helping people achieve their professional goals through job placements, transfers, promotions, etc. The odds of Larry and I showing up in that lobby at the same time and the same day after not seeing each other for almost a year were unbelievably small, and yet there we were hugging each other and welcoming each other to our new job. I thanked God for giving me this gift on my very first day, my first hour back to work. To be greeted by a friend, and friend no less who was very happy to see me and grateful for my help, was a spectacular way to start my new job assignment.

My host made it to the lobby to pick me up, and it was an engineer whom I had worked with and who had worked for me numerous times over the last twenty years. A skilled tradesman himself, a millwright, Tom had started working as a contractor for GM many years ago and helped follow the installation of projects. A faithful and honest man, Tom is a good friend, and I was so happy to see him as well. Wow, I thought, this coming back to work is great. I am seeing friends and reliving shared memories and getting paid well in the process. I had left a very good job with a lot of security, plunging headlong into a life that I did not know how I would proceed with, and God was giving me far more than I could have ever asked for. We can never outdo God in His generosity I had been told, and I was seeing how true that statement really was.

As I started to reorient myself into the work routine, it all came back pretty quickly. The beauty of my new assignment was that I was free to work on the things that I most enjoyed. Instead of spending a lot of time in meetings, which I understand are necessary but can be unbearably tedious, I was able to spend time out on the assembly plant floor looking at the equipment as it was installed and ensuring it was functional and safe. In addition, I had the opportunity to work with so many people I had built relationships with in the past. Most everyone wanted to talk to me about what it was like living the life I had chosen. Did I miss the job, did I enjoy doing what I was doing? I always replied pretty much the same thing, I did not miss the job but really missed the people I had worked with. Now, I was able to work for just a few months a year, got to see all the people I had been friends with over the years, and got to work on some challenging assignments.

One thing I learned was that as we go through our careers, really take time to listen and engage the people you work with to understand them and get to know them more personally. If you are like most people in the USA, you spend at least as much time with your coworkers as you do your family. Over the years, these relationships you build with your coworkers will help you when work gets difficult or if you are forced to look for another place to work. These friendships build networks of colleagues who you may be able to help down the road or who may be able to help you. Also, truly listening to your coworkers with the ear of your heart, truly hearing what they have to say will build relationships that will last a lifetime.

As the end of my first contract assignment since retiring was about to end, I was a bit bittersweet about it. I had enjoyed greatly working with my friends again, but after working a lot of hours in a short amount of time, I had become a bit burned out again. My heart goes out to those who are still early in their careers and have, what seems to them, a lifetime ahead of them of long hours and unfulfilling assignments. With mortgages to pay and children to raise, the tough reality of getting up early every morning and going to a job that you may not enjoy is difficult. If you are able to choose a line of work that you enjoy as you are getting out of high school or college, it makes the years ahead of you much more bearable from a professional perspective. I always tried to keep in mind when work was rough and I was struggling, how fortunate I was to, firstly, have a job and, secondly, have one that paid me pretty well. So many hardworking people around the world are underemployed due to circumstances beyond their control. Many others work much harder than I ever did and are paid a fraction of what I made, again due to circumstances beyond their control. If you ever get the feeling that your job is just terrible, but you have limited choices, be thankful for the God-given ability to work and to have a job that pays you so much more than many other people around the world make. We are truly blessed in the United States to have all that we do. Our challenge is to balance the material possessions that we are told every day in the media we must have with the reality of what is really necessary and the time we should spend with our family. True happiness has never and will never come from the things we buy but from the people we love and those that love us.

I continue to be so fortunate that I am able to somewhat pick when and where I want to work. For now, my wife and I will continue to live as simply as we can, try to minimize our costs so that we can do "real work" for just a short time while spending the bulk of our time experiencing the beauty of nature that God has created and volunteering and giving back for all the blessings we have received.

Volunteering

After our year or so of traveling the country in our RV, we had always planned to spend a good bit of our time doing volunteering opportunities. The first big volunteering experience we had was moving onto the monastery grounds with the Benedictine sisters at Mount St. Scholastica monastery in Atchison, Kansas. Arriving in mid-May of 2019 and planning to stay until the end of the year, we thought this experience would give us almost eight months of living simply and prayerfully within the community of sisters.

When we arrived at the Mount, we had been communicating with Sr. Loretta, the volunteer coordinator, about our travel plans and arrival dates. As we got close, we kept in touch and let her know the day and approximate time of our arrival. When we finally rolled onto the monastery grounds with our semitruck-length RV and trailer, we parked in one of the numerous parking lots and looked around at our home for the rest of the year. Though we had been here many times before, the beauty of the Mount and the grounds always impressed and inspired us. As we made our way to the volunteer house where we would be living, we got lost a few times on the very large campus. After walking into houses that were occupied by other sisters, we finally found our way to our new home. We would be living in Marywood hall for the rest of the year. We slowly walked up the steps of the century-old house and found a nice handwritten welcome note to us taped to the front door. As we walked in, several sisters were waiting at the kitchen table to greet us and welcome us home. We felt like part of the community from that moment forward. The sisters were welcoming and kind and so grateful to have us at the Mount. We always expressed to them how grateful we were for being allowed to live here, and they would quickly say that it was they who were thankful for us being so loving and caring of the community.

After spending the first few days getting settled in, we decided we would wait until the start of the following week to dig into our new volunteer roles. We took the first few days to unload our RV and make ourselves at home in our new abode. It was a real adjustment moving from an RV with about 350 square feet of living space into the huge old house that was Marywood Hall. Built in the late 1800s, the place was absolutely palatial in comparison to what we had been living in for the last year. With seven bedrooms and five bathrooms, there was ample space for the three residents living there. Besides Tami and I, there was one other volunteer that lived in the house. Having a bedroom that was more than half the size of our RV certainly allowed us to expand our living space and comfort zones. Over the time we lived at Marywood, we always kept in our minds that at the end of the assignment there, we would have to move back into the RV and that we could not start a lifestyle of acquiring things again. It is amazing how quickly the desire to buy things comes back once you have room to store them. Living in the RV was nice because we just didn't have room for more stuff. Living in a large house was a great exercise in focusing on prayer and life experiences and not getting joy out of buying new and fancy stuff.

Getting settled in and comfortable, we were ready to earn our keep by volunteering. As with most long-term volunteering assignments, we were given free room and board in return for our time. So, in return for our volunteering, we got to live in this beautiful house, had all our meals provided, and were able to join the community in prayers and mass each day. While not making the money I would have if I had stayed in the corporate world, or any money for that matter, I was doing something I very much enjoyed by helping the sisters and was, maybe, building up my treasures in heaven. I had no need of a job that paid me large sums of money. I had worked enough over the past few months to cover my bills for the year, so now I was free to do what I wanted, and helping this community was what I wanted to do.

After a few weeks of figuring where help was really needed and for the community to see what I was capable of doing, I sort of settled into a fairly regular routine. On Mondays and Fridays, I would help Sr. Elaine and Sr. Rosann with the numerous tasks they were responsible for related to facilities maintenance and landscaping. I quickly became best friends with the nice gas-powered industrial type weed whacker they had here. I could, and often did, spend a full eight hours a day applying the high-speed nylon string at the end of the weed eater to the out-of-control grass that grew over each sidewalk and around the cemetery. At the end of the day, I had accomplished much, or so I thought, but had finished less than a quarter of the grounds here. Once the temperatures heated up and the landscape grew less like a rainforest and more like a midwestern lawn, we were generally able to keep up. In truth, it was all I could do to keep up with Sr. Elaine. Slightly older than me, she was an incredibly hard worker, and I tried hard to help take as much work off her plate as I could. Once we had gotten the weeds and landscaping somewhat under control, the next big assignment was to clean all the fan coils in the AC and heating units throughout the monastery. Built in the late 1800s, the monastery did not have a big central heating and cooling system installed into it when it was built. Over the decades, the heating and AC units that you may have seen in hotel rooms were added throughout the monastery. Though providing the sisters much-needed heating and cooling, these units required maintenance to clean and swap out the filters. Individually, it was not a lot of work. But due to the hundreds of them throughout the monastery, it was a task that took us months to complete. As the last one was done, I was overjoyed to be done with that task.

On Tuesdays in the morning, I had the opportunity to chauffer the sisters around town. As the sisters had gotten older, many needed rides to the doctors or to the store, and I was able to help them with that. It was a bit of break from the hard work on Mondays and gave me the opportunity to get to know many of the sisters much better. I really enjoyed hearing about their life experiences and all the different things they had done and people they had influenced. The sisters were and are truly inspirational people. Throughout their lives, they shared their knowledge and wisdom with many students, worked in health care, and provided a loving touch to so many people. All the while, they kept God and His love at the center of their hearts while selflessly serving so many others.

In addition to the wisdom they shared, the sisters were also great storytellers. Sr. Thomasita told me about the time an elderly sister had started to lose her memory, and she would wait in the dining area for each sister as they entered for meals and tell them that she loved them, regardless if she could remember them exactly or not. Sr. Thomasita asked her, "Why do you tell them you love them before you are even sure who it is?"

The aging sister replied, "I used to have some enemies, but I have forgotten their names now." What a wonderful attitude to have, I thought. Instead of wondering who it was you might have held a grudge against, just give in to the love for all that is pulling at your heartstrings.

Another epic story was from our volunteer coordinator from the time she worked in the lower income area of Kansas City at a place called Peace House. Peace House was a house where many sisters lived while they worked at the school across the street or did other ministry in the greater Kansas City area. Like most big city mission locations, the area was a bit rough, but as this is where the need is, this is where the sisters go. One evening many years ago, Sr. Loretta was closing up the school and walking back across the street to Peace House for the evening. Her mother happened to be in town and was with her that evening. As Sr. Loretta looked back at the school, she noticed that one of the windows had been broken and was open. Bothered because she was due to be back home to help prepare the meals, she obligingly returned to the school, unlocked the door, and went in to see what was going on. With her mother behind her, rosary in hand as they walked through the halls, they turned the corner to see a big tall young man in the hallway. Without panicking or calling for help, this was in the time before mobile phones, Sr. Loretta approached the young man who towered over her and asked him what he was doing in the school. Making up a story that she immediately sensed to be nonsense, Sr. Loretta confronted the man and told him she did not believe him and told him to show her how he had gotten in and what he had taken. Slowly they walked down the stairs into the basement. What a group, a large young man followed by Sr. Loretta and her elderly mother, now not just clutching the rosary but reciting each step of the way. Into the dark basement they went, and sure enough, she could see where he had broken in. "You're going to come back here tomorrow and clean this up," Sr. Loretta instructed the intruder without hesitation. Her fierce Irish heritage coming to the surface, she was letting him know who was boss and what he was going to do. Slowly, and menacingly, perhaps meant to intimidate the women in his presence, the young man lifted his shirt to reveal a large knife he was carrying in his pants. Without missing a beat, Sr. Loretta exclaimed, "And you stole my favorite knife as well. You put that down on the table right now, and we are going to walk upstairs." Incredulously, the young man, apparently stunned at the force of nature he had encountered, did as instructed and put the knife on the counter and slowly walked back upstairs. He did not return the next day to clean up his mess, likely afraid of the wrath he would incur if he were to show up again.

Back to the schedule I had developed. On Tuesday afternoons, I would often spend those few free hours after driving the sisters around cleaning the fleet of cars they had here. Much to my chagrin as a retired General Motors employee, of the thirty or so cars they owned, I would guess about twenty-five of them were foreign from a large Japanese manufacturer. I gave the sisters some good-hearted ribbing about buying American, but with the blurred lines between what is domestic and what is foreign, it's really hard to push that too much these days. The cars were cared for by Sr. Sharon. Sr. Sharon was in her mid-eighties and yet chauffeured on some days and helped maintain the cars on others. Driving them to the shop for repairs and making sure they were cleaned to her standards, she was a marvel of the "get it done" attitude.

My idea of aging and what can be done by older citizens really changed during my time at the Mount. It is proudly, although somewhat cautiously, said by the sisters here that the Mount is managed and maintained by a group of sisters mostly in their midseventies or older. It was not uncommon to see seventy-year-old or older sisters riding the lawnmowers around the property, getting on their hands and knees and helping me clean fan coils, maintaining the fleet of cars, and many other things. There are sisters in their early nineties who walk miles each day and go to the local jail for ministry. There are sisters in their late nineties that still paint the icons that adorn the walls of the monastery. In the bulk of American society, when people get to this age, they become very sedentary and literally rest on their laurels, if they are not in wheelchairs or if they even make it to this age. Perhaps it was the balance of their lives between prayers and work, the healthy food they ate, or the joy they had from living in a community they loved, but these sisters seemed healthier and more active than any other group I had ever met. It was an instructive experience for me about the true value of a balanced life.

Wednesday was my day to help with housekeeping. Though there is a paid housekeeping staff here, there is so much to do that many of the items that aren't regularly required to be done like cleaning bathrooms and vacuuming the floor often go long periods without being done. These tasks, like cleaning windows and buffing floors, are the things I was able to help with. I can say without reservation that I cleaned more windows in my time at the Mount than I had done for the total of my life up to that point. The windows were fun to work on because the results we immediate and impactful. The sisters were so grateful for these small tasks. I was thanked every day for it. I found great joy in doing these small, simple tasks that brought so much happiness to the people that were affected by them. It was not rocket science or solving difficult challenges; it was just doing simple tasks that no one else had time for, but it really made a lot of people happy.

Thursdays I kind of carved out my own time to write, to go to the gym, and to tend to personal tasks. It took me a long while to understand it was okay not to work twelve hours every day trying to get everything done. It was okay to stop before a task was fully complete so I could get to the chapel in time for morning, afternoon, or evening prayers. The Benedictine motto of Ora et Labora, prayer and work, was on my mind and my lips each day. I worked hard for the times when I worked, but I made sure I had time to pray, time to write, and time to care for myself physically by going to the gym and running. This is the balance that I had never had, and it was a difficult lesson to learn.

During the week, I developed a pretty solid routine. Arising at 4:45, I would be in the Scholastica chapel each day by 5:30 to say my rosary. This powerfulness and joy that this experience had on me was enough to get me out of bed each and every day at that early hour. Arriving in this huge and beautiful chapel each morning while it was still dark out and having the entire chapel to myself was overwhelming to me. I would walk slowly up to the very front pew and say hi to Jesus, Mary, and Joseph. It was as if my family was waiting for me each morning. I would then settle into the pew and spend the next thirty or forty minutes praying and thanking God for everything He had given me and asking for prayers for my family and friends, for vocations and numerous other things. It was a powerful way to start each day.

After finishing my rosary, which is unique in how I say it, I would walk down the monastery hall just a few hundred feet and join the community for morning prayer at 6:30 a.m. in the choir chapel. Usually thirty minutes long, it was a wonderful way to start the day with the community as we prayed, chanted, and sang each morning as our offering of thanks to God. Finishing around 7:00 a.m., we would take a fifteen-minute break to grab a quick coffee or glass of orange juice before gathering again in the chapel for daily mass at 7:15 a.m. A priest would come over from the abbey each day and say mass where we would hear from the Gospel and the readings of the day and partake in the Eucharist. To be able to receive the real body and blood of Christ each and every day to sustain me on my journey was a powerful way to begin my day. Perhaps it was this daily substance of the body of our Divine Father that provided the longevity to so many sisters in community. By 8:00 a.m., I had spent the first two and a half hours of my day in personal and community prayer and was ready to start the day. This was the balance I had never had in my life prior to this point.

As I reflect, I can say that my heart was bursting with love and gratitude during my time at the Mount. I would talk with my family and friends and tell them I couldn't believe how absolutely blessed my life was. I was surrounded by amazing, caring, and loving people, and I held no malice, anger, or resentment toward anyone in my life. I think it was taking this time each day to start my routine with prayer and reflection that allowed me to be so open to this gratitude. I took time each day to thank God for everything I had. When each day I am thanking Him for blessings instead of complaining about work, about money, or about all the other things I used to worry about, it makes sense that your heart becomes full of love and gratitude. While most people are not able to carve two or three hours out of the start of their day in this manner, just a simple ten or fifteen minutes to start is all that is required to readjust our gratitude levels. Spending that time thinking about all we have been given and all the people we love and who love us really helps us to remember what is important and to dismiss the little things that can seem so big if we let them.

Death in Community

One of the most moving and revealing experiences I had while volunteering at the Mount was to participate in a funeral service at the passing of one of the sisters. During my time at the Mount, six sisters passed away. I was deeply moved by how the community came together to gather around the sister as she neared the end of her time here on earth. There were sign-up sheets posted on the bulletin boards to get volunteers to sit with the sisters each hour as their time of passing neared. These sheets were never on the board for more than an hour or two before they were completely filled up with volunteers for hour by hour visitation for the next several days.

Often when one thinks about religious people, men or women, leaving their family and joining a community of nuns, monks, or whatever, we think about all they are giving up with their family and having children, etc. What I have found has been the total opposite of that. Having done hospice care for many years, sadly I was often the only one to visit my patients. They would go days with no visitors excepts doctors or nurses that did not have time to just sit with the patient and be present for them. In a community like the Mount and other religious groups, the sisters and brothers are surrounded by people who love them and have shared their life experiences with them. It was a very moving experience to see the love that all the members of the community had for their soon to be departed sisters.

Once the sisters did pass, the ceremony was a true celebration of their life. Family and friends would attend the prayer vigil on the evening before the funeral, and after prayers, everyone would gather in the dining area. Stories would be told by sisters about their experiences with their beloved sister who had just passed. The stories were touching, heartfelt, but mostly hilarious recitations of a life well lived. Though there was some sadness at not seeing their sister anymore, there was great joy in knowing that their sister was basking in the divine light of God's presence. Without exception, these vigils and gatherings afterward were always a joyous celebration of their sister's life. It was because I was allowed to share in these gatherings and was asked to be a pallbearer at one of the funerals that I was truly able to understand what a blessing it is to be able to live in a true community of lifelong friends and colleagues.

Journeying into Love

Our journey here on earth is never complete until we breathe our last gulp of air. There are always roads to explore, people to meet, love to share, and lessons to learn. I had been raised in fractured family with little material goods in my youth and had learned much of what I understood as a man, as a father, and as a husband through trial and error, mostly error. With little paternal direction in my youth, my ideas of what a man was and wasn't and the role that God played in those roles took me decades to even begin to understand.

As my journey deeper into His love continues, I am blessed to be surrounded by amazing friends and family. The friends I have made over the last ten years as I have begun this journey of love have lifted me up and taught me more than I could have hoped to learn about true love and growth. I will continue to try to make time each day for prayer, meditation, and deep listening.

In a time in American history where our society is so divided and full of anger, it is critical to keep my heart open to love, forgiveness, and understanding of other people's perspectives. If someone attacks my ideals or beliefs in such a manner that it becomes personal, I pray I will always have a heart of love to see them as a fellow brother or sister of God and that I may not let anger surround my heart and draw me to seek to lash back at them. Truthfully, I feel like I have been so blessed that I rarely if ever find myself in these situations anymore. Through the choices that I have been fortunate enough to make through the smallest slice of God's wisdom, the people that surround me now seek to lift me up and share their love with me as well.

In the year ahead, my wife and I have already been asked to spend several months in Europe volunteering with another religious community in Ireland. I have general plans of what the future year may hold, but as with everything, they are subject to how the Spirit moves and my discernment of God's plan for my life. Thomas Merton's famous poem about trying to discern God's plan for our lives comes to mind,

Thomas Merton's Prayer for Discernment

O Lord God,
I have no idea where I am going,
I do not see the road ahead of me,
I cannot know for certain where it will end.
Nor do I really know myself,

And that fact that I think
I am following Your will
Does not mean that I am actually doing so.
But I believe
That the desire to please You
Does in fact please You.
And I hope I have that desire
In all that I am doing.
I hope that I will never do anything
Apart from that desire to please You.
And I know that if I do this
You will lead me by the right road,
Though I may know nothing about it.
Therefore I will trust You always
Though I may seem to be lost
And in the shadow of death.
I will not fear,
For You are ever with me,
And You will never leave me
To make my journey alone.

This poem has always spoken to me very powerfully. I do not know for sure if the road I am taking is what God really wants for me. But I think He knows that I am trying to discern the path, and even if I make a wrong turn due to lack of wisdom or prayer, He will guide me back to the path, whatever it may look like. Where this path will lead, I do not know. I only know and trust that if it is illuminated by light of God's love, the journey will be memorable.

ABOUT THE AUTHOR

Martin Rymarz wrote the bulk of this memoir of his journeys and his lessons learned while living and volunteering at a Benedictine Monastery in Atchison, Kansas. Having retired from the corporate world at a relatively young age, Martin and his wife gave away their possessions, purchased an RV, and spent their days, when not volunteering, traveling the country and exploring nature.

Martin studied for four years at Sacred Heart Major Seminary in Detroit, Michigan, pursuing his master's degree in pastoral administration with a focus on health care. As part of the degree requirements, Martin worked for three years as a hospice care volunteer and interned as a hospital chaplain in a busy Detroit area hospital. The lessons from these experiences helped form Martin, and many are captured in this book. Alternatingly fascinating, somber, and humorous, these experiences working with people at their most desperate times taught Martin valuable life lessons of faith and love.

As a retired manufacturing engineering manager from General Motors, Martin's technical expertise in the industry allowed him to travel the world for his job and interact with people of all faiths and socioeconomic backgrounds. These work colleagues, who would become close friends of Martin, also altered his perception of world cultures. Seeing the world through the eyes of these friends instead of the lens of a news camera was life-changing for Martin.

Martin and his wife have four adult children. Being the second marriage for both Martin and his wife, lessons learned from raising children, divorce, parenting from a distance are all shared in this book.